Easy Woodstuff
for Kids

Easy Woodstuff for Kids

By David Thompson

Illustrations by Stacy Buhler

Gryphon House, Inc.
Mount Rainier, Maryland

© **1981 by David T. Thompson**

ISBN 0-87659-101-2

Library of Congress Catalog Card No. 80-84599

Design by Cynthia Fowler

Dedicated
to the spirit of
my mother

Acknowledgements

To **Arthur Carpenter** for being the master woodworker that he is.

To my Father, **Ellsworth Thompson**, for his interest and encouragement.

To my friend, **Seth Harding**, for his wisdom, aid, and understanding.

To my editor, **Carol Reynolds**, for her excellent efforts in editing the original manuscript. Without her help the book would not be what it is.

And to many wonderful children, whose inspiration made this book possible.

Sita Harding
Ari Harding
Alicia Douma
Heather Garaway
Steven Rosenthal
Justin Rood
Thomas Billingsley
Karen, Susan, Diane, Robin, James, Melany, Joseph Thompson

Table of Contents

Introduction 11
Safety 13

Sources and Resources 15
Measurements
The Work Table
The Hammer
The Hand Drill
The Back Saw and Miter Box
Clamps
Glues
Sanding
Painting and Finishing

Sticks Are Made of Wood 35
Write Your Name With Sticks 38
A Scroll Made From Two Sticks, A Piece of Heavy Paper,
Sticks and Leaves 40
A Birdfeeder Made From A Stick And A Piece Of Scrap
Wood 42
Frame Your Favorite Picture 44
The God's Eye Or Ojo 46
Religious Symbols From Around The World—Trees Of
Life 48

Branches on the Tree of Life 51
A Holiday Centerpiece/Candleholder 54
A Pencil Or Crayon Holder From A Branch Of A Tree . . . 56
A Key Holder And A Christmas Tree Ornament 58
A Necklace Or Decorative Pin 60

Two-By-Four Art 63
A Two-By-Four Wall Hanging 66
A Two-By-Four "Knick-Knack" Shelf 68

Scrap Wood Projects 71
A Wooden Trivet Made From A Piece Of Scrap Wood . . . 74
A Tic-Tac-Toe Game From One Piece Of Scrap Wood . . . 76
A Tray Made From A Piece Of Scrap Wood And A
Clothesline 78
A Musical Sand Block 80
A Musical Wooden Cymbal 82
Bookends Made From Two Pieces Of Scrap Wood 84
A Note Holder Made From A Piece Of Scrap Wood
And A Clothespin 86
A Japanese Serving Table Made From Three Pieces Of
Scrap Wood 88
A Letter Holder Made From Three Pieces Of Scrap
Wood 90

Plywood Projects 93
A Tray Made From Three Pieces Of Plywood 96
A Photo Hinge 98
The Magic Broom Holder 100

Three Advanced Projects 103
A Flowerpot Holder 106
A Birdhouse 108
A Tool Box 112

Introduction

My first woodworking teacher was my grandfather. He had a shop in his garage and would spend most of his days there. I soon found that his shop was an interesting place. Later I had a good shop teacher at the YMCA. While most kids were in the gym or playing pool, I was in the shop.

Later in life, when a new generation arrived, little ones would ask, "What is David making?" I soon realized why my grandfather enjoyed having me around. It is fun to do things with children. They are alert and ready to learn. One day I was working on a Christmas gift in my father's workshop. I had returned home for the holidays after having been away for a while. My niece, Karen, came bouncing down the stairs. "Uncle David, what are you making? Can I help you?" I said that I was making a bandsaw box (a box cut with a bandsaw from a single block of wood). We sanded the various pieces of the box and glued them together. It was a wonderful experience working with a child. She wanted to know what kind of tree the wood came from, why we put oil on the wood, and what a bandsaw was.

Some years later I was visiting some friends who had young children. Anticipating seeing them, I had cut out some pieces of wood so that the children and I could make something. Two children made a hobby table, another made a cradle for her doll, and a five year old friend made jewelry for his mother from small pieces of wood. At each household I was struck by the joy children have in making something from wood. I started to think about writing a book that would share with parents and teachers some of the fun of doing woodwork with children. I hope you will have as much fun as I did.

Within each chapter are several projects, each one using similar materials and techniques. I've arranged the book so that an adult can work through it with a child, or select projects at random. There are enough projects so that a teacher can introduce one project per week for the entire school year.

The book is arranged so that the simplest projects are at the beginning. They use the most available materials: often sticks that can be picked up in the park or the back yard. Later projects use small peices of scrap wood.

In all of the projects, I've tried to take into account several things: the cost of the project, its utility and beauty, the availability of materials, the simplicity of the project, and the applicability of the project to a home or classroom setting. In a real sense, I see the book as a woodworking primer not just for children, but for all of us.

The tools used are the hammer, the ruler, the hand drill, the back saw, the miter box and clamps. The back saw and the miter box can be used by children if the adult feels that they can handle them. Otherwise, these tools can be used by the adult with the children watching. I know children will want to use the saw, and I have found it possible for them to use it if they agree to follow directions very carefully. There is a section in the book explaining the use of the tools along with suggestions about how to choose tools for children.

Some of the projects involve using power tools in the preparation of materials. If power tools are not available, there are resources that can be tapped. If you are a parent, perhaps this is the time to try out a new power drill. If you are a teacher, a local high school shop might be a resource.

I'd like to say thanks to each of you who use this book. It is an experiment, and all of us who use it are experimenters. If you have any comments or suggestions, I'd like to hear about them.

Safety

Protect the hands,
Protect the children,
Protect them from being harmed.

Over and over we must talk about care and caution. Children move quickly. Their hands move from one thing to another before we can see them. They have to be slowed down. Part of our role is slowing them down, making them conscious of what they are doing, and giving them the opportunity to do something slowly, carefully and deliberately. The tools used in this book have been limited to those that will not easily harm a child. But all tools can injure someone if used improperly.

Besides limiting the tools that are used, the stage must be set for an injury-free experience. Before starting a project, I like to settle everyone down and make the children aware that I will stop whatever is going on at any time I feel that tools are being used unsafely. I find that it is helpful to follow a regular pattern in introducing tools, and to always give a child a moment or two to calm down before using a tool.

When an injury does take place (this usually involves the need for removing a splinter or a hammer hurting a finger), I tell the injured child what to do about it and then direct the child to where first aid can be found. If the child has a splinter, instructions are given to go get the fingernail clippers (which I keep in a convenient place) and I will help remove the splinter. Then I tell the child to go run cold water over the finger. If a child hits a finger while hammering, cold water is immediately run over the injured finger while the child is told to think about why the injury occurred. I try to be consistent in always giving primary responsibility for taking care of the injury to the child.

In addition to the cold water treatment, it is mandatory to have a first aid kit. A bottle of mercurochrome and bandages are good for open wounds.

Sources and Resources

The high school shop teacher and students are an extremely helpful resource in preparing materials for young children. Every school district has a high school shop, and most shop teachers with whom I talked have been eager to help in the preparation of materials. One shop teacher said that helping with these projects was "just what I was looking for." His beginning students did much of the preparation for many of the projects included in this book.

It is important to develop a relationship with the shop teacher. Bring this book and visit him and his class. Describe what you are doing and ask for his help. In each of the project descriptions there is a section that tells exactly what is needed in the preparation for the project.

It may be possible for your class to visit the high school shop, or to have the shop teacher visit your class. Perhaps some students from the shop class can be enlisted as aides.

Another readily available resource is the local lumber yard. Still another is the cabinet shop. In these places, scrap wood abounds. Although wood is very expensive and smart shopkeepers try mightily to conserve as much as possible, there are always scrap pieces that can be given to worthy causes. I am certain that you will find more scrap wood than can possibly be used in your projects.

If there is a building site in the area, there will be enough scrap wood to supply many projects. Most of the "short end" pieces are thrown away or burned. Ask the children to bring in wood, and have a box where they can put it as they bring it in. One small piece of wood can be a project to a child.

Friends can be helpful. I know because I am one of those "helpful friends." Often people collect several do-it-yourself tools and then do nothing with them. Show them this book and enlist their aid. People really like doing projects, but they often don't dream up projects on their own. You have the projects, they have the tools. What a fit!

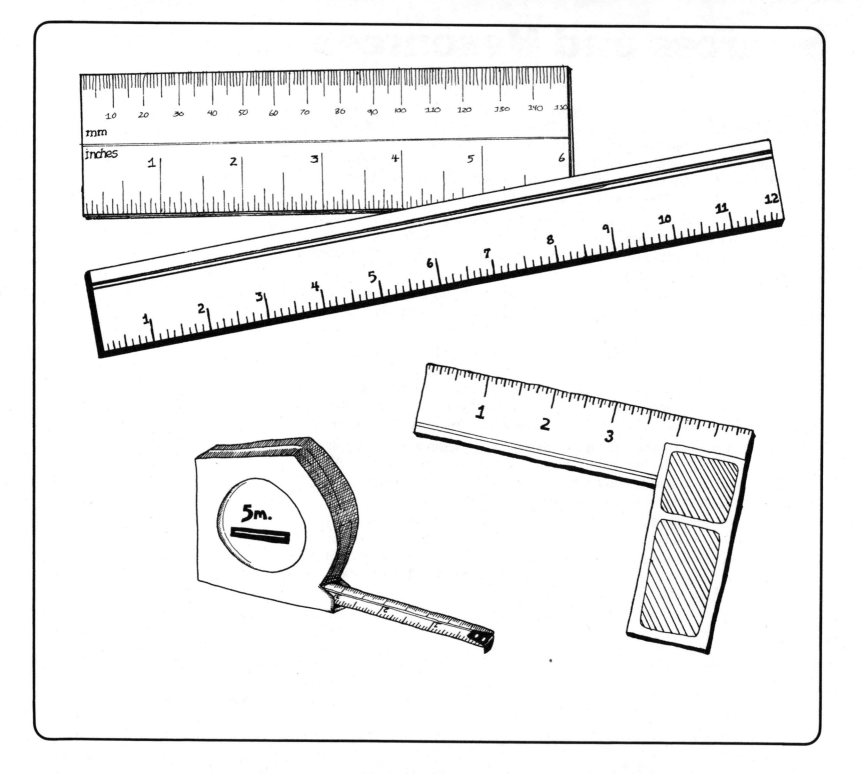

Measurements

With the exception of the final three projects, exact measurements are not imperative. The word "approximately" preceeding measurements means that the exact measurement is not critical to the success of the project. More important is the relationship between measurements: length to width; width to height.

All of the projects are measured in two systems: the *English System* (inches, feet, yards), and the *Metric System* (millimeters, centimeters, meters). If something is five inches in the English system, it is 12.7 centimeters in the Metric system. To facilitate easy measuring, I have rounded numbers like this one off to their nearest whole number—in this case 13.

Three measuring tools are good to have: a **Ruler** which gives both the English and Metric measurements; a **Tape Measure** (some of these also have both measuring systems on the same tape); a **Try Square** (or carpenter's square) which is an excellent tool for measuring and drawing right angles.

Work Table

In order for children to do good work with wood, they need a good place to work. A sturdy table is very important. The ideal height is "knuckle high." With arms at one's sides, the table should be level with the knuckles of the child's closed fist. At home you may want to shorten the legs of an old kitchen table. The projects in this book do not call for elaborate work benches or vices. If you will be working on a table that is used for other things, you will want to protect its surface with a piece of wood.

Hammer

Children love to hammer, but in order to hammer well, they need a good hammer. The average hammer weighs about 16 ozs. (454 grams). This is too heavy for children. Unfortunately, most hammers made for children are of inferior quality. When purchasing a hammer, make sure you get one that is light enough for children to handle. Look for one that weighs between 8 and 10 ozs. (227 and 284 grams). Price is a fair guideline to follow in looking for a hammer. Other things to look for include the *face*—it should be smooth with no pit marks or dents; the *handle*—it should be small enough so that a child can get his or her hand around it; the *claw*—it should have sharp edges which come to a definite point. This allows the removal of small nails.

In hammering there are three principles to follow:

•First, grip the hammer two to three inches from the end of the handle.

•Second, keep your eye on the head of the nail. Tap the nail with the hammer until it is securely in the wood. Then move the helping hand away from the nail and hammer with a more forceful motion.

•Third, use the wrist as the main force when hammering...not the elbow or shoulder. The more relaxed the arm, the easier it will be to hammer accurately.

A valuable method for keeping the fingers away from the hammer when using small nails is to use a piece of heavy paper or light cardboard, pressing the nail through it. This can then be held where the nail is to be hammered. Otherwise, the fingers are too close to the hammer. Since I learned this, I have not once hit my fingers!

If the nail is not hit squarely, it will bend. When this happens, use the claw of the hammer to remove the nail. Insert the claw under the head of the nail and push away from the nail. A block of wood placed under the head of the hammer will add leverage and protect the wood from which the nail is being pulled.

If you can find an old stump, use it for a hammering practice place so as not to waste pieces of wood which could be used for projects. Since the nails will be going into the end grain, they will usually go in without bending.

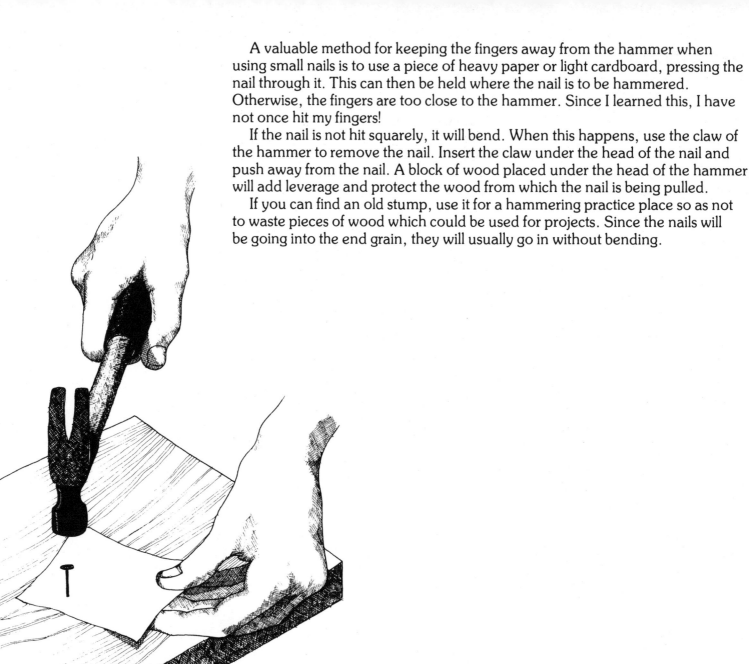

20

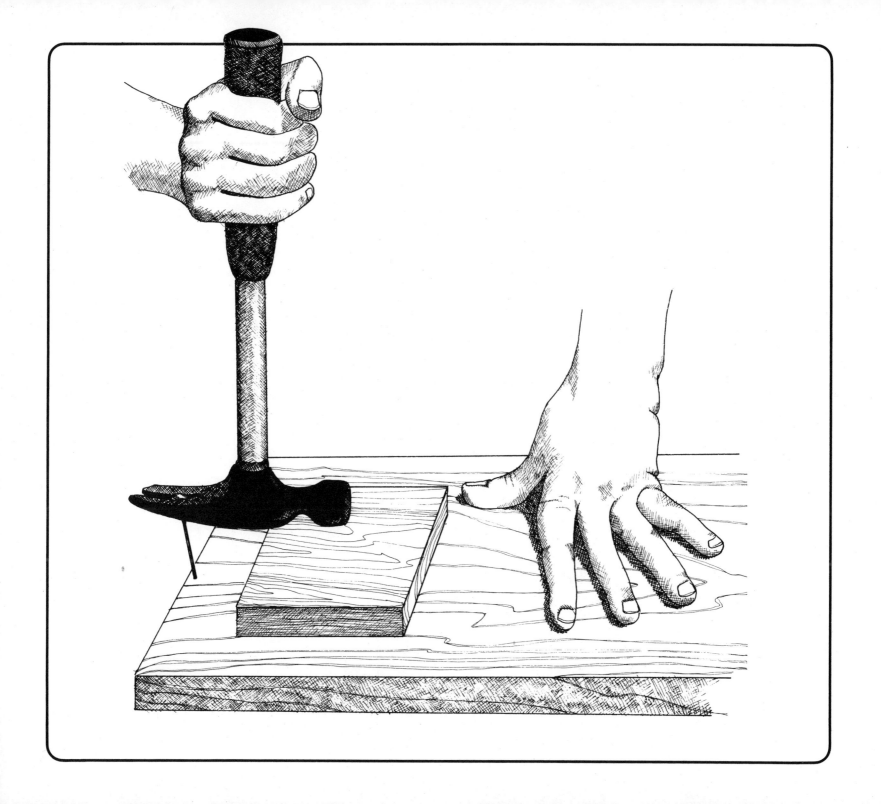

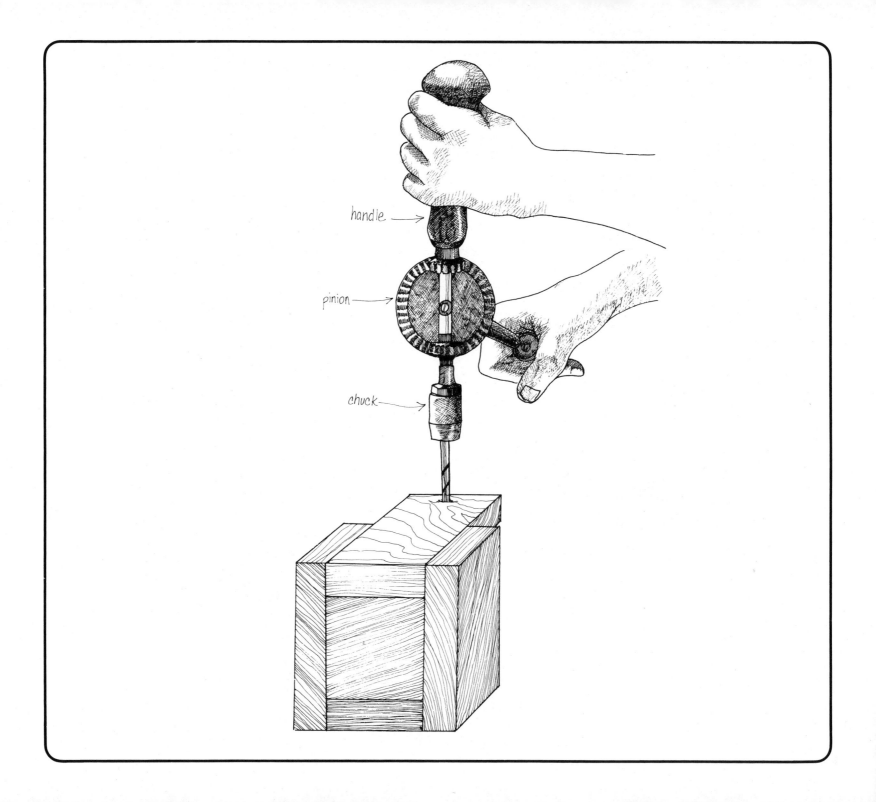

handle

pinion

chuck

The Hand Drill

The hand drill is another good tool for children who are beginning to work with wood. I made the mistake of giving my discarded hand drill to a five year old friend. He found it to be as useless as I did. There is no substitute for a good tool.

There are several good hand drills on the market. The one I like has a removable cap on the handle to store various sizes of drill bits.

The hand drill has three principal parts: the *handle*, the *chuck* and the *pinion*.

When putting a bit in the chuck, hold the pinion in one hand. Put the bit in the chuck. Hold the chuck tightly with the other hand. Then turn the pinion counterclockwise. The jaws of the chuck will close, tightening against the bit. To remove the bit, repeat the process, but turn the chuck clockwise. Children will need the help of an adult in inserting and removing bits from the drill.

When drilling, secure the piece being drilled to a table or bench, using a clamp.

To start a hole, use an awl or large nail to make the "starting hole" on the mark where the hole is to be drilled. Then put the bit in the starting hole and begin drilling. Have one hand on the main handle and the other on the handle of the pinion. Hold the drill straight up and down and try to get a smooth movement into the drilling. To remove the drill and bit, continue drilling in the same direction while pulling the drill upwards and out of the hole.

Another stump can be used as a practice place for drilling. Make sure there are no metal objects in the stump as they will tend to dull the bits.

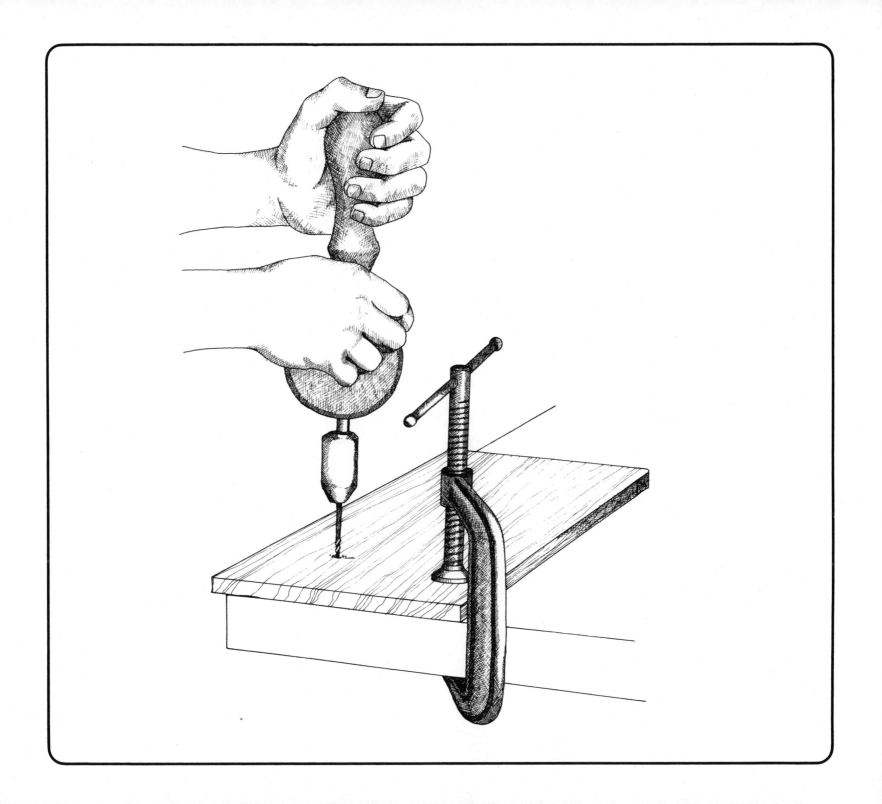

The Miter Box & Back Saw

The **Miter Box** is generally made of hard wood (although some plastic ones are also available), and has two sets of grooves cut into it—one for sawing straight lines, and the other for sawing 45 degree angles. It is an inexpensive and useful tool to have. I use it with children because it insures that lines will be cut straight. Also, the grooves in the box insure that the back saw cannot move in any direction other than backwards and forwards. When using it often, I like to secure it to the work bench or table.

The **Back Saw** is a fine toothed saw used for cutting wood across its grain. It has the added feature of having a heavy piece of metal along its top edge which greatly strengthens it. It easily fits into the grooves of the miter box, and, if sharp, will cut small pieces of wood easily. The saw should always be stored in a place where it will not touch any other metal object. Otherwise, the saw will become dull in short order.

When sawing a piece of wood, place it in the miter box and either hold it or clamp it securely. The back saw is then inserted into the grooves and moved back and forth with the effort on the push stroke. Let the saw do most of the work. Try not to put too much pressure on the saw as it can bind. If this happens, lift the saw and start over again.

CHILDREN SHOULD NEVER BE ALLOWED TO USE THE SAW WITHOUT ADULT SUPERVISION.

Clamps

Clamps are used to hold pieces of wood together while the glue between them dries. They are also used to hold pieces of wood to the work table while they are being sawed, drilled or nailed. The clamp used in the projects of this book is called the "C" clamp, so named because of its shape. It is a handy tool and very important to the safety of the children. A good rule to follow whenever drilling a hole in a piece of wood is to clamp it to the work table. A clamp is like an extra hand, and a very strong hand at that. If the clamp is used it means that we have two hands with which to work.

Clamps come in different sizes. For the projects in this book, four inch (10cm) clamps will work best.

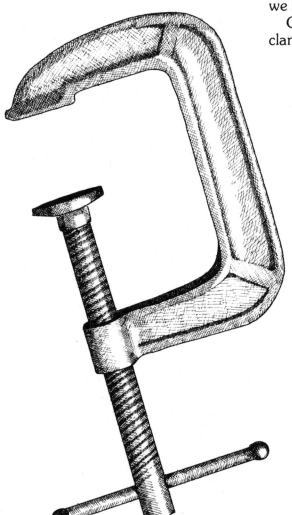

Glue

There are a number of good glues available, however for the projects in this book I have limited them to three: Rubber Cement, White Glue, and Yellow (or Aliphatic Resin) Glue.

Rubber Cement generally is used for joining two pieces of paper. It is a well tested product with which most of us are familiar. The important thing to remember in using rubber cement is to apply it to both pieces of material being joined. No clamps or weights are necessary.

White and **Yellow Glue** are similar with one important distinction: white glue is not resistant to water but yellow glue is. So if something is made that may be out of doors for a long time, use yellow glue. Either glue should be applied to both pieces of material being joined. The two pieces are then nailed, clamped or weighted until dry. Before the glue dries, any excess can be wiped up with a damp rag. Drying time varies, so read the instructions on each container. Generally it is wise to let the project dry overnight before using it.

The yellow glue dries quite quickly. I'd suggest using this glue when affixing sticks to cardboard and clamping or holding is impossible. Be sure to put lots of glue on each of the sticks.

Sanding

Sanding a piece of wood brings out the quality of the grain. There are several grades or "grits" of sandpaper. The *coarse* one is 80 grit. The *medium* is 120 grit and the *fine* is 220. Sheets of sandpaper are approximately 9" x 11" (23 x 28cm). For most projects, fold the sheets of sandpaper into four parts, then tear the sheets into separate sections. For some of the projects the sandpaper can be torn into even smaller sections.

Often a sanding block made from a small piece of wood is used to sand flat surfaces. Fold the sandpaper around the block and begin sanding with the grain of the wood. Be sure that the piece of wood being sanded is either held or clamped to a table or bench.

If you want to make the object being sanded even smoother, switch to a finer grit sandpaper. It is surprising how beautiful the grain in almost any piece of wood can be when sanded smooth.

When sanding, I often sing a song. It seems to make the work easier and more enjoyable. I often make up sanding songs with children. An example of one to the tune of "Row, Row, Row Your Boat" goes like this:

Sand, sand, sand your wood
Looking at the grain,
When you think your work is done,
It's time to start again.

Painting and Finishing

You may want to paint or varnish some of the projects to enhance their beauty and/or protect the wood. Unfortunately, most of the products available are not easy to use with children. The only way I have devised to easily varnish projects is to use a cardboard box approximately 18" (45cm) square, and cut off the top. I put the project(s) to be finished inside the box and, using a spray can of varnish, put a finish on it. This, of course, is *NOT* something children should do.

When finishing projects such as necklaces that need to be varnished on both sides, let the one side dry, then turn them over and spray the other. There are a lot of driers in the spray can varnishes, so they dry almost immediately upon contact.

To obtain a highly polished finish, it may be necessary to put more than one coat of varnish on the project. If so, lightly sand the project with fine sandpaper between coats.

In the classroom it is possible for children to use water paints to finish some of their projects such as the musical instruments or the bookends. The paint will crack and peel off in a short period of time, but the paint can be removed by washing the project in water. If you are working with one or two children, perhaps you may want to attempt using a latex based enamel. This kind of enamel can be cleaned with water. But like all paints it can be messy and will surely become a part of the children's clothing by the time they are finished.

I would suggest that you read carefully all the information on the cans of paints and varnishes before using them.

BE SURE THAT THERE IS AMPLE VENTILATION IN THE AREA WHERE YOU ARE USING THEM.

**Sticks Are
Made
Of Wood**

Sticks Are Made Of Wood

Sticks can be found all around us: sticks from elm trees, redwood trees, maple trees, pine trees or other varieties, can be used in the projects in this chapter. They are beautiful, useful and free for the collecting.

Parents and teachers can encourage children to collect sticks of various sizes...dry them, store them, love them and learn from them.

The projects in this chapter show several useful, fun and beautiful things that can be made with sticks. I'm sure that you will find more. Each time I do one of these projects, the children teach me something new.

Some of the projects can be done with little or no supervision. If you try the projects yourself before introducing them to the children, you will discover which projects will need your attention and which can be done by simply placing the materials and a sample of the project before the children.

Have fun and remember that in addition to teaching our children how to work with wood, we are teaching them about loving trees.

Guardians of our children
Guardians of our forests
We learn as we love.

Write Your Name With Sticks

This is a project for children who know the letters in their names. They can make a picture of their names by using two sizes of sticks.

Materials

Pieces of cardboard approximately 5" x 12" (13 cm x 30 cm)
Straight sticks approximately ¼" (5mm) in diameter cut into lengths of 3" (8cm) and 1½" (4cm)
Glue
Cord

Tools

No tools are necessary for children.

Preparation

It is advisable to have the cardboard and sticks cut to their proper size before introducing the project to the children. Garden shears will do the job quickly. After the sticks are cut to size, put them in two boxes or bags to separate them by size.

If you want the children to cut their own sticks, show them the two sizes to be cut, then let them break the sticks into their proper size. It is not so important that the sticks be of the exact measurement as long as they are of two distinct sizes.

Instructions

1. Write the child's name in bold letters on the piece of cardboard, or let the child write his/her own name on it.

2. Find the sticks that make up the letters of the child's name. Some children will need help making the letters B, G, P, R, S because round letters must be squared.

3. Put glue on the sticks and arrange them on the cardboard.

4. Set the project aside to dry.

5. Punch two holes in the cardboard and tie the cord for hanging.

Comments

Leaves can be glued to the cardboard as decoration. This is especially appropriate if the leaves come from the same kind of tree as the sticks.

Variations of this project can include using sticks of differing shapes. Where a stick branches in two, a "Y" or "V" or "W" or "M" can be found. Often a "J" or "U" can be found in a curved part of a stick.

This project can be incorporated into an outing. Children can find their own sticks and leaves, discover which leaves and sticks come from the same tree, and look for different shaped sticks. After the project has been completed, a box of sticks can be collected and cut so that they are ready when a child wants to repeat the project.

I've found that children love this project. They are fascinated with the challenge of making letters out of sticks. Later in the book this project is repeated making shapes and symbols.

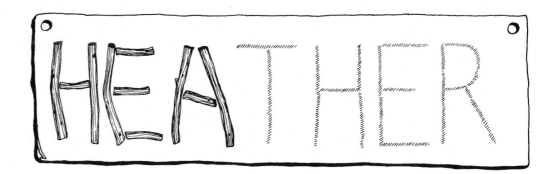

A Scroll

Made From Two Sticks, A Piece Of Heavy Paper, Sticks And Leaves

This is an easy project suitable for children three years of age and older.

Materials

Two sticks 10" x 12" (25 to 30cm)
Heavy paper 9" x 14" (23cm x 35cm)
  Either brown wrapping paper or paper
  from grocery bags will work well
Leaves, cones, small sticks for decoration
Cord
Glue and Rubber Cement

Tools

Back Saw
Miter Box

Preparation

A collection of sticks, leaves, seeds, small cones and other appropriate material may be put together in advance, or children might gather it on a nature walk. For young children, an adult should cut the sticks to size. Children four and older can probably, with help, cut their own sticks to size in the miter box.

Brown paper should be collected and cut to size. I've found that the paper in grocery bags works well in this project. Perhaps each child could collect one paper bag.

Instructions

1. Fold the paper and glue it 1½" (4cm) below the top and bottom folds.

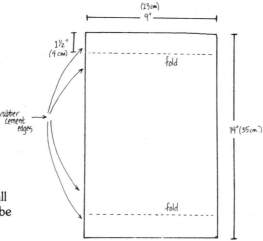

2. Place a leaf, a cone, and a stick on the paper. Move them around. Find a good design. When you are satisfied with the design, glue each piece to the paper.

3. Set the project aside to dry.

4. Cut the sticks and insert them in the folds of the scroll.

5. Attach the cord and it is ready to hang.

Comments

Variations of this project are many. Older children can do a study of an oak tree by finding a piece of bark, a leaf, a stick and an acorn. Other children can paint a picture of their favorite tree on a piece of paper and then make it into a scroll. Someone else might find a picture of a forest in a magazine and glue it to the paper. There are a lot of things to do with this project. Like the last project, this one would be good to incorporate into a nature walk. I like to take a few things from a particular kind of tree and show them to the children. Then I ask the children to find a tree that has the same kinds of things. They soon find out that acorns don't come from chestnut trees and that there are a good number of different kinds of bark on trees. Perhaps the children can find a young and old tree of the same type. When they look at the bark, they will see how it changes with age.

A Birdfeeder
Made From A Stick And A Piece Of Scrap Wood

This is a simple project using the miter box, the back saw, the hand drill (optional) and the hammer. In addition to providing a nice way to feed birds, it teaches children how to find the center of a piece of wood.

Materials

A stick about ¾" to 1" (2 to 2.5cm) in
    diameter, cut 10" (25 cm) in length
A scrap piece of wood approximately
    6" x 10" (15cm x 25cm)
A nail 1½" (4cm)
A small screw eye
Cord

Tools

Back Saw
Miter box
Hand drill—¼" (5mm) bit (optional)
Hammer
Pencil
Ruler

Preparation

You might want to ask children to bring in scrap pieces of wood and have a scrap box where contributions can be deposited. If you plan to purchase wood from a lumber yard, ask for 1" x 6" (2.5cm x 15cm) fir or pine. This can be cut easily into useable pieces. I've found that building several sizes of birdfeeders makes a more interesting project than making them all the same size.

Sticks need to be collected. Show the children the size stick needed (see materials section) and have them find one that is the same size.

Instructions

1. Cut the stick to size in the miter box. Children will need help with the saw, so it may be wise to have the sticks cut to size before-hand, or the adult can demonstrate how to cut the stick while the children watch.

2. Using the ruler and pencil, draw diagonal lines on the piece of scrap wood.

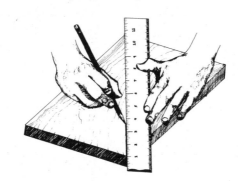

3. Hammer a nail through the scrap wood where the diagonal lines intersect.

4. Hammer the nail with the wooden piece attached into the end of the stick. Here is where two children can help one another. One child may hold the stick while the other hammers, then they may change tasks.

5. Screw a screw eye into the top end of the stick, tie a cord through it and it is ready to hang.

Optional

You may want to drill a hole through the stick 1" (2.5cm) from the top, using the hand drill, then tie a cord through the hole and the birdfeeder is ready to hang.

Comments

It's been my experience that once children make one of these, they will want to make others. Later in the book there is a simple design for a birdhouse. But in the meantime there are many variations on the design for the birdfeeder. You could nail sticks to the sides of the piece of scrap wood. This gives the birdfeeder a more rustic look and adds variety to the project. Or you could use an old pie pan, using it as the base and nailing a stick to it in the same way as described in the instructions for this project.

Frame Your Favorite Picture

This is a simple project for children of all ages. It can be either a beautiful gift or just something nice to have.

Materials

Cardboard pieces 11" x 11" (28cm x 28cm)
Sticks approximately ½" (1.5cm) in diameter
  cut to lengths of 10½" (27cm)
Glue
Sandpaper
Cord

Tools

Back Saw
Miter box

Preparation

Cardboard will have to be collected and cut to size. I'd suggest selecting a standard size, say 11" x 11" (28 x 28cm). You may want to cut the sticks to size before they are introduced to the children. If you have plenty of time, let the children use the saw to cut their own sticks. If you decide not to have the children use the saw, you or someone else will precut the sticks. If the cardboard pieces are 11" x 11" (28 x 28cm) the sticks will be 10½" (27cm). You may want to have children bring the sticks in as they are collected. Show them a sample of the size of stick needed for the project. Perhaps you can display them and have the children measure their sticks to those on display.

Pictures will have to be collected. The children could bring in a picture of themselves, their parents, their pet dog, or a favorite picture they have drawn.

Be sure to cut the sandpaper into small squares so the children do not waste it.

Instructions

1. Glue the picture to a piece of cardboard.

2. Cut the sticks to size.

3. Sand the ends of the sticks.

4. Glue the sticks to the edges of the cardboard.

5. Set the project aside to dry.

6. Attach a cord and it is ready to hang.

Comments

Although this is a simple project, it teaches some valuable skills and introduces a new concept that will be expanded upon in later projects. This is the first project where sandpaper is used.

The concept that is introduced is the arrangement of material of the same size. Notice that the sticks are all one size and form an interlocking design.

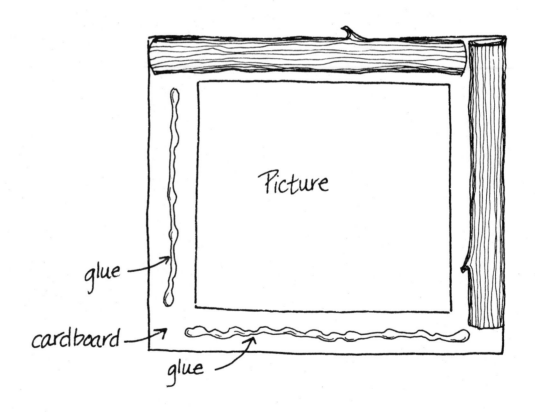

glue

Picture

cardboard

glue

The God's Eye, Or Ojo

This is a beautiful symbol of Huichol Indian prayer. The crossed sticks symbolize the four directions: North, South, East, West

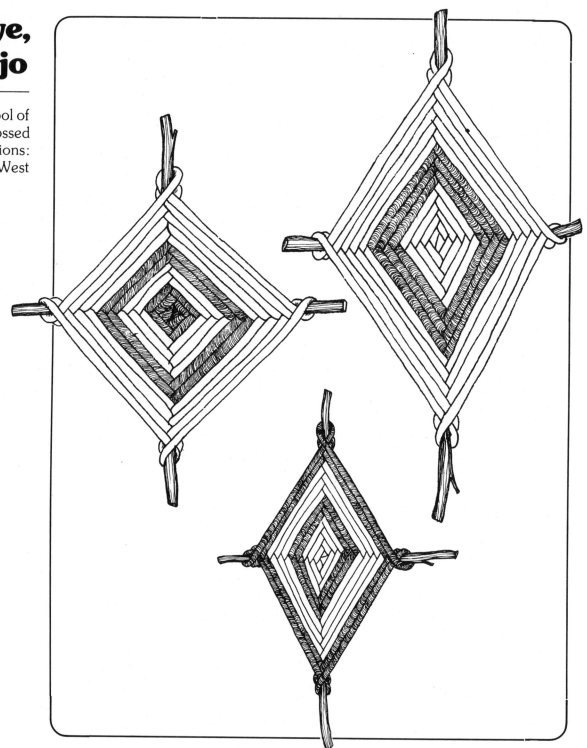

Materials

Sticks, about the diameter of a pencil, 6" to
   8" (15 to 20cm) in length
Different colors of yarn
Glue

Tools

Scissors

Preparation

Several different colors and thicknesses
of yarn should be collected. Sticks will need
to be collected and dried. Perhaps you could
make several God's Eyes and let the children
examine them before making their own. This
may be the time for a lesson on Huichol
customs. There are several good books to
choose from, some with vivid pictures of
Huichol art.

Instructions

1.   Use some yarn and tie the sticks
together. Then put some glue on the yarn
to keep it in place.

2.   Start the yarn at the center of the
cross. Tie it securely, then "weave" the yarn
around the cross, going over and around
each stick. Be sure to keep the yarn tight.

3.   If you want to change the color of the
yarn, tie the new yarn to the old and continue
weaving.

4.   To finish the God's Eye, tie the yarn
to one of the sticks and put some glue on
the back side where the yarn touches the
sticks.

Comments

It takes a while for children to learn how
to do this project. But after they discover how
much fun it is to make these symbols, they
will want to make them again and again.
Gluing and tying the sticks together before
the children start helps to get the project off
smoothly.

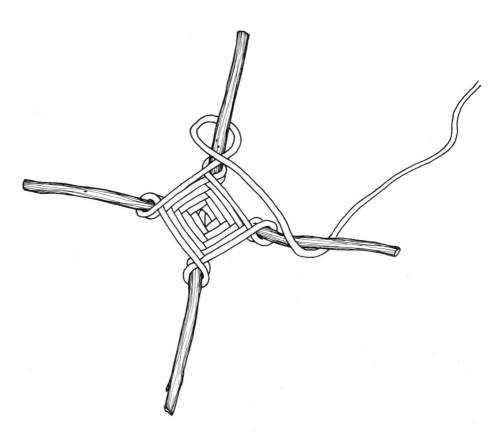

Religious Symbols

From Around The World—Trees Of Life

Based on what the children have learned in this chapter, they can enjoy making any or all of these symbols. They can also invent symbols of their own.

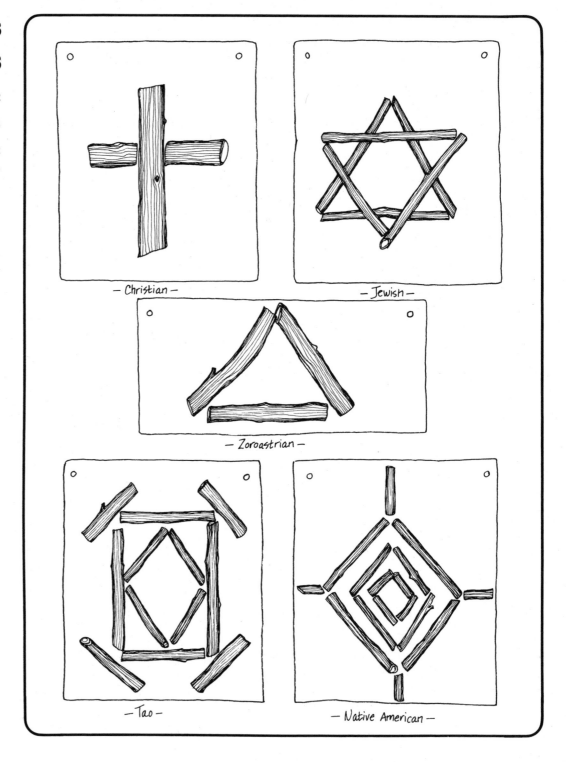

— Christian —

— Jewish —

— Zoroastrian —

— Tao —

— Native American —

Materials

Sticks, about the diameter of a pencil
Cardboard pieces
Glue
Cord

Tools

No tools are necessary for this project.

Preparation

This is a simple and enjoyable project. You will want to prepare different sizes of cardboard. A good size might be 6" x 6" (15 x 15cm), however this can vary. Sticks will have to be collected. If you don't have a stick collection, have children collect sticks that can be broken by hand. The best size is the diameter of a pencil.

You may want to talk about different religions and the significance of their symbols. The drawings included here represent but a few of the many religious symbols of the world.

Instructions

1. Show the children different religious symbols.

2. Have each child pick out one or two symbols. Draw the symbol on the piece of cardboard, or have the child draw the symbol.

3. Choose some sticks, break them into proper sizes, put glue on them and arrange them on the piece of cardboard.

4. Set the project aside to dry.

5. Punch holes in the cardboard, put cord through the holes and it is ready to hang.

— Hindu + Buddist —

— Islam —

— Hindu —

— Hopi —

49

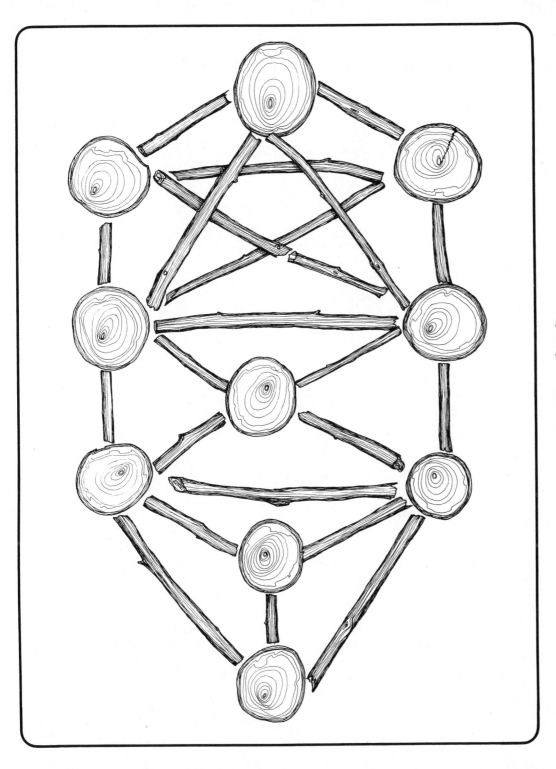

**Branches
on the
Tree of Life**

Branches On The Tree of Life

In this chapter we discover some very interesting ways that branches (or fallen limbs from a tree) can be used in woodworking projects. As before, we are using parts of the tree in their natural form—not wood that has been milled and cut up into shapes. I feel it is important to stress in these beginning chapters a need for wood conservation.

The projects in this chapter are simple, exposing the beauty and utility of the branch as it is exposed. Using small pieces of the branch, candle holders, pen and crayon holders, pins, and necklaces are made.

Sanding is an important part of this chapter. It may be a good idea to review the section on sanding and to prepare some sanding blocks to be used by children in several of the projects.

All of the projects will be beautiful without adding a varnish or oil finish to them. I have not included instructions on finishing in the project descriptions because often it is more bother than it is worth. There is a section on finishing in the front of the book if you want to use it with any of the projects. Once you become familiar with the process of finishing, I think it will be possible to attempt it with small groups of children.

As an introduction to this chapter, I've used sticks and branches to draw the atomic structure of carbon, which is known to chemists as being the basis for all living things. In the ancient Jewish tradition of the Kabbala, it is also used to symbolize a system of higher spiritual attainment. Both of these symbols—which are identical—are referred to as the Tree of Life.

A Holiday Centerpiece Candleholder

This is an easy project, suitable for four year olds.

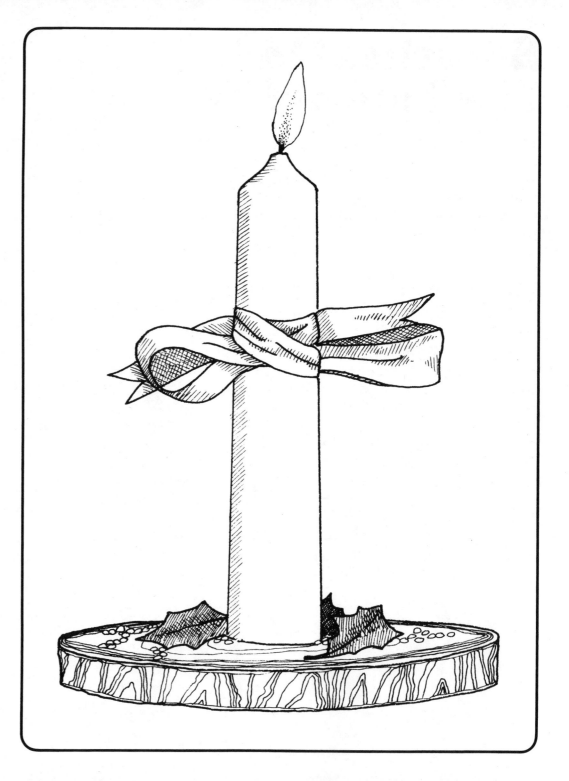

Materials

Pieces of a branch 4" to 6" (10 to 15cm)
 in diameter, ¾" (2cm) thick
Candles (Emergency Candles work well)
Glue
Aluminum foil
Nut shells, seeds, and dried berries

Tools

No tools are used by children. (See
preparation section.)

Preparation

Slices of wood have to be cut from a tree's
branch. Most kinds of trees are suitable,
however, "green" pieces (those cut from a
branch that was recently alive) tend to split.
The actual cutting can be done with a hand
saw but involves strenuous work. It is a good
idea to enlist the aid of someone with a band
saw. With power tools the preparation for this
project is very simple.

The slices of wood should have a hole
drilled in the center, half way through them,
the size of the diameter of a candle. If you
have an electric drill, a ¾" (2cm) "speed-
bit" can be purchased inexpensively. But if
you are a teacher with lots of holes to drill,
I would suggest that the local high school
shop class be asked to do the preparatory
work.

Nutshells, seeds and berries have to be
collected. A bag of birdseed contains
interesting and beautiful seeds.

Instructions

1. Put some glue on the piece of wood.

2. Arrange the nutshells, seeds and berries
on the wood.

3. Wrap a piece of aluminum foil around the
candle and place it in the hole.

Comments

The aluminum foil wrapped around the
candle acts as a fire barrier. I used to do this
project without using the aluminum foil. One
day a child told me that his candle holder
caught fire. From that day on I changed the
project so that it did not create a fire hazard.

A Pencil or Crayon Holder
Made From A Branch Of A Tree

This is a simple project using wood from a fallen branch.

Materials

Pieces of a branch 2" to 3" (5 to 8cm)
   in diameter, cut into 4" (10cm) lengths.
Sandpaper—80 grit
Small pieces of fabric
Glue

Tools

Sanding block
Scissors

Preparation

Read the preparation for the Holiday
Centerpiece project. Cut the branches into
lengths and drill holes in the top of them.
These should be about 3/8" (1cm) in
diameter and about 1½" (4cm) in depth.
For some of the holders you may want to
drill several holes, and for others only two.
I have found that for a pencil holder, two
holes is enough, but for crayons it is better to
have up to six.

You will want to collect some scrap
material to glue to the bottom of the holder.
Felt is best.

Instructions

1. Sand the holder on the top and the bottom
using the sanding block. Make sure that the
wood is smooth.

2. Place a piece of fabric under the holder
and trace around it.

3. Cut out the piece of fabric.

4. Glue it to the bottom of the holder and it
is ready to be used.

Comments

If you would rather use scrap pieces of
2x4's instead of the branches, the same
project can be made with them.

57

A Key Holder And A Christmas Tree Ornament

This is a simple project that uses a thin slice of a tree's branch. The project also teaches children how to sand a piece of wood.

Materials

A branch 1½" to 2" (4 to 5cm) in diameter cut into discs approximately ¼" (7mm) thick.
Key chains or ornament hooks
Sandpaper—80 grit
Masking tape

Tools

Back Saw (See Preparation)
Miter box (See Preparation)
Hand drill—3/16" (5mm) bit
Sanding block

Preparation

One branch will be ample wood for several projects. Find a fallen branch and allow it to dry for several days. The ends will undoubtedly crack, but there should be enough wood in the interior of the branch for the project. The pieces of wood, or discs, can be cut in a miter box with the hand saw. (However, the children will not be able to saw this size branch.) As a demonstration, perhaps you could cut a few with the children watching. The rest should be cut with a bandsaw as it will take a good deal of time and effort to do it by hand. That friendly high school shop teacher could help by having a student practice cutting the pieces. (Be sure to tell whoever does the cutting that if the chips are over ¼" (7mm) in thickness, they stand a chance of splitting.) After the chips are cut, it is good to dry them for a day or two before proceeding with the project. Otherwise the wet wood will gum up the sandpaper.

Key chains or ornament hooks will have to be purchased. Key chains can be found at drug stores or hardware stores and are inexpensive. Ornament hooks can be found at drug stores during the Christmas season. I've found paper clips bent into an "S" shape also work well.

80 grit sandpaper will have to be purchased. Four to six pieces can be cut from one full sized sheet.

Sanding blocks will have to be made or purchased. Check the section on Sanding for instructions on proper sanding technique.

Instructions

1. Take a piece of masking tape. Wad it up and stick it to the work table. This provides a non-skid surface to hold the chip while sanding.

2. Put the chip on the tape.

3. With the sanding block and sandpaper, sand the chip. Keep a smooth action in the sanding, and sand in only one direction.

4. Turn the chip over and sand the other side.

5. Place the chip on a block of wood with another wad of tape under the chip.

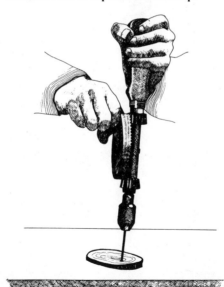

6. Drill a 3/16" (5mm) hole about 3/8" (1cm) from the edge of the chip.

7. Put the key chain or ornament hook through the hole and it is ready to use.

Comments

Notice that no finish has been put on the chip, and that only one piece of sandpaper was used. In the next project we will use three grits of sandpaper.

Finishing the chip with varnish or oil brings out the color and beauty of the grain and protects the wood. I use it with groups of two or three children all the time. However, I am reluctant to suggest your using it if you have a number of children working on a project at the samed time. Varnish and linseed oil are petroleum based materials, very harmful if breathed or swallowed. They are not products that you want children to handle. If you want to put a finish on the chip, use lemon oil or other plant based oils. These are not toxic, so can be used by children. They will not harden, so the oil will have to be applied regularly to keep a luster on the chip. Re-read the section on *Finishing* for complete instructions on the various materials used to finish a piece of wood.

A Necklace Or Decorative Pin

This is another project that uses a slice of a branch to make jewelry.

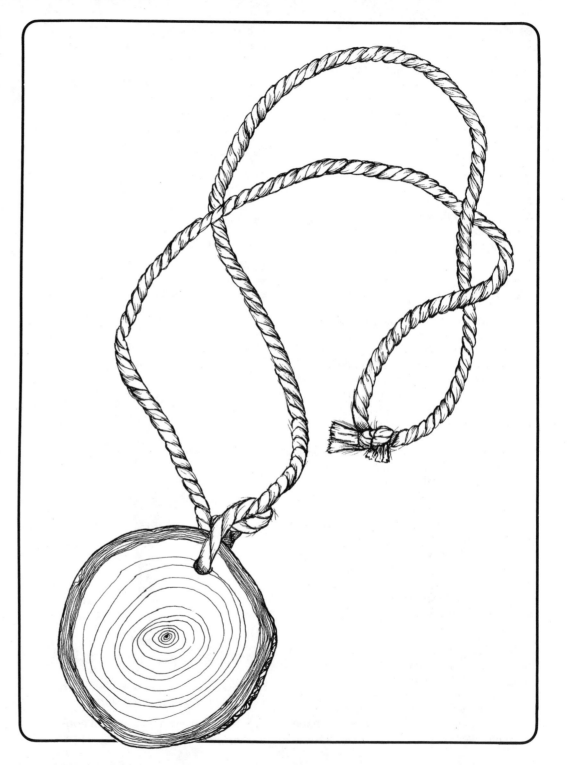

Materials

A branch 1½" to 2" (4 to 5cm) in diameter
   cut into "chips" approximately ¼" (7mm)
   thick.
Leather strands
Pins
Masking tape
Sandpaper—80, 120, 220 grit

Tools

Back Saw
Miter box
Hand drill—3/16" (5mm) bit
Sanding block

Preparation

For a complete description of what to do to
get the slices prepared, read the section on
Preparation in the KEY HOLDER project.

Leather strands will have to be purchased.
They can be found in a hobby or leather
shop. If you can't purchase leather, cord
works well and is easily available. The
decorative pins that attach to the wood can
be purchased at a hobby shop or ordered
through a hobby or crafts catalog and are
inexpensive. I have used pins from discarded
costume jewelry and have found them to
work well. I have also used discarded cuff
links and glued small pieces of wood to them.

In this project, three grits of sandpaper
are being used. Each sheet will have to be
cut into smaller pieces so that it will not be
wasted. (See the chapters on **Sanding** and
Finishing.)

Instructions

1. Take a piece of masking tape. Wad it up
and stick it to the work table. This provides
a non-stick surface to hold the chip while
sanding.

2. Put the chip on the tape.

3. With the sanding block and sandpaper
(80 grit) sand the chip. Keep a smooth action
in the sanding and sand in only one direction.

4. Turn the chip over and sand the other
side.

5. Now repeat the process using the next
finer grit sandpaper (120). Notice how the
finer grit removes the scratches left by the
previous grit. Don't go on to the next grit
until all the scratches are removed from the
previous grit. While you are sanding, sing
some songs.

Here is a song sung to *Row, Row, Row Your
Boat*:
   Sand, sand, sand the wood,
   Looking at the grain.
   When you think your work is done
   It's time to start again.

6. Before sanding with the finest grit (220),
I ask the children to moisten the chip to see
how beautiful it looks when wet. This also
raises the grain and makes the chip very
smooth after the final sanding. The more
times the chip is sanded, the more beautiful
it will become.

7. If you are making a necklace, place the
chip on a block of wood, with a wad of
masking tape under the chip.

8. Drill a 3/16" (5mm) hole about 3/8"
(1cm) from the edge of the chip.

9. Put the leather strand through the hole
and it is ready to wear.

(If you are making a pin, glue the pin to the
back of the wood chip. Let it dry and it is
ready to wear.)

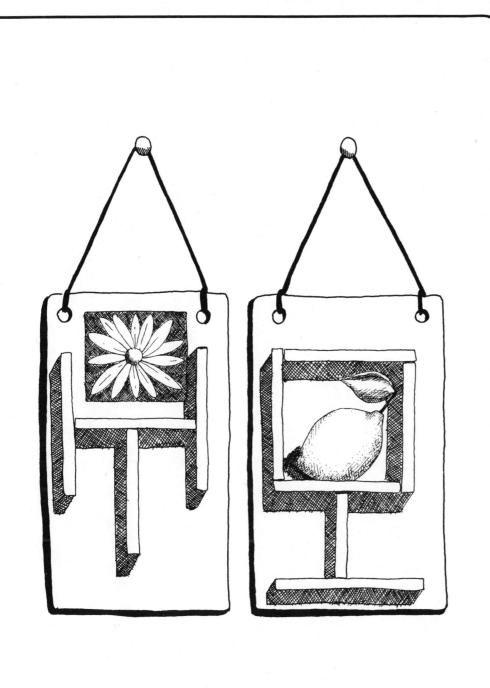

**Two-
By-Four
Art**

Two-By-Four Art

Two-by-four art is something I discovered by accident. Having completed a woodworking project, there was a lot of scrap wood around that I didn't want to discard. I started playing with the shapes that the "end grain" made. By looking closely at the end grain I could actually visualize the tree that created the board. I could count the rings in each board which signify the age of the tree. Each light area separated by a darker area signifies the growth of the tree.

I cut out some wood chips and found all sorts of intricate grain patterns. In some of the chips I found knots—or slices of knots—where a branch grew from the trunk of the tree. Looking at these knots I could imagine lions, birds, owls and human forms.

One day, while working on a project with a group of children, a little girl started gluing the chips on a board. Since she was gluing them in a manner unlike the instructions I'd given, I asked her what she was making. She told me she was making a shelf to put in her room. This was the beginning of a new set of projects. Later another child used sticks and chips together, making a hanging pencil holder.

In cutting out the chips, I prefer using a power saw. This, of course, is done before the project is introduced to the children. The older the piece of wood used, the more beautiful it appears to be. A table saw, skill saw or band saw can be used to cut out the chips. It takes very little time and effort, and will result in some very interesting projects.

I've done these simple projects many times and have never tired of them. I hope you and your children will also enjoy them. They make excellent gifts for children to give to friends and relatives.

A Two-By-Four Wall Hanging

A project suitable for young children
to hang in their own room.

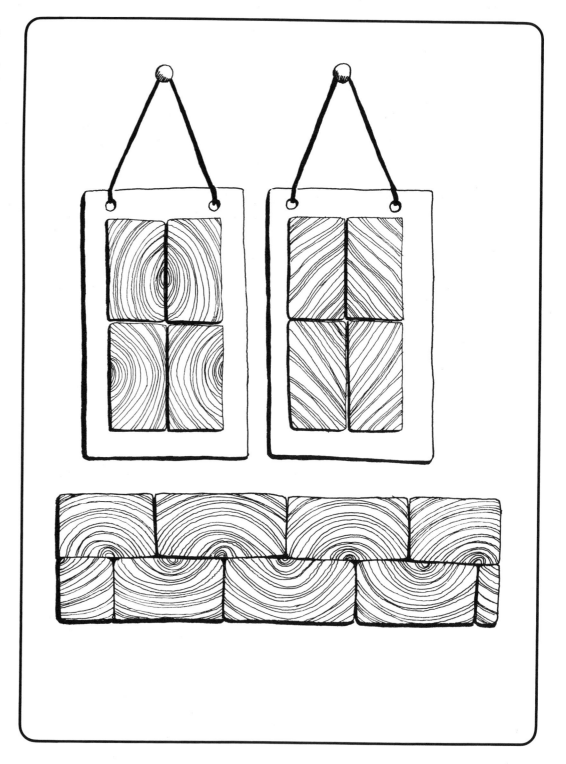

Materials

¼" (7mm) thick 2 x 4 "chips" (See chapter
  introduction)
Cardboard pieces
Glue
Cord

Tools

No tools are needed

Preparation

2 x 4 chips will have to be cut from a 2 x 4
board. (See chapter introduction.) One
standard size board will produce enough
chips for several projects. As I mentioned in
the introduction, I like to use old discarded
2 x 4's. There is something about the quality
of the grain that makes the old ones more
beautiful.

Cardboard will have to be collected and cut
into different sizes.

Instructions

1. Use several chips. Look at them and see
if you can make a circle, a diamond, or an
oval shape with the grain of the chips.
Perhaps you can make a zig-zag pattern.

2. When you have found a pattern you like,
glue the chips to the cardboard. Try to center
them and keep them evenly spaced.

3. Set the project aside to dry.

4. Punch two holes in the cardboard, tie a
cord through the holes and it is ready to
hang.

Comments

This is a simple project, but one that
results in a beautiful wall hanging. If you
would like to "dress up" the cardboard, cut
colored paper to the size of the cardboard
and glue the two pieces together before
adding the chips. In examining the chips
that come from the 2 x 4, you will often see
a slice of a knot that may look like something
familiar. Put two together and they may form
the eyes of a bird or animal. There are all
sorts of beautiful patterns to be found in these
pieces of wood.

A Two-By-Four "Knick-Knack" Shelf

A simple "hang-up" shelf that can be made by small children to hold their own collectibles.

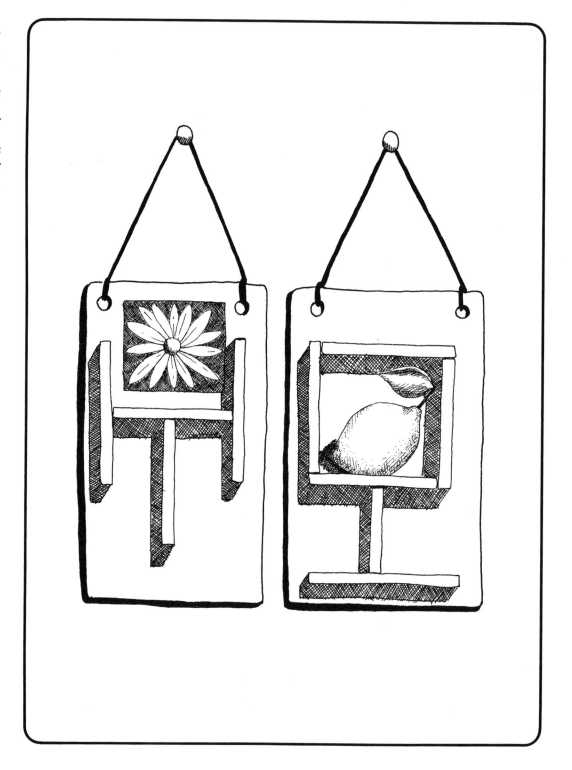

Materials

¼" (7mm) thick 2 x 4 chips
Scrap pieces of wood for backing,
    approximately 6" x 9" (15cm x 23cm)
Glue
Cord
Attractive pictures

Tools

Hand drill—3/16" (5mm) bit
Scissors

Preparation

If you had enough chips cut out for the last project, there will be very little preparation for this one. Look over the Preparation section of the TWO BY FOUR WALL HANGING project for directions on how to prepare the chips for this project.

Scrap pieces of wood will have to be collected.

Old magazines or greeting cards can be collected, as some children will want to decorate the project with them.

Instructions

1. Use several chips. Arrange them on the backing to form an interesting pattern that can be used to hold something. When a pleasing pattern has been found, put some glue on one edge of the chips and glue them to the backing. Children may need some help in lining up the chips.

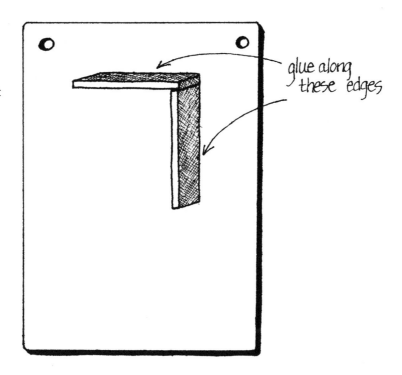

glue along these edges

2. Cut out a picture to decorate the shelf. Glue it on the backing.

3. Set the project aside to dry.

4. Drill two holes in the top of the backing. Put some cord through the holes and it is ready to hang.

Scrap Wood Projects

Scrap Wood Projects

In this chapter, one, two, and three pieces of scrap wood are used. From these scraps, trays, tables, musical instruments, book ends and note holders are made. All of the projects involve using standard one inch (25mm) boards, (which due to lumber industry standards are actually three-fourths of an inch [19mm] in thickness). The boards that are used are all "soft" wood, making it easy to hammer a nail. The term soft wood generally refers to Pine, Fir, or Redwood.

In each of the project descriptions, I have included exact measurements for the pieces of wood. Often you will find that it is not necessary to follow the exact measurements that I have given. They have been given as examples of relationships between sizes of wood more than as strict measurements to be followed. Since the projects are made from scrap pieces, I'm sure you will find interesting pieces that can be used in all sorts of ways.

In some of the projects, hammering is important. There is a section on hammering which gives the basis for this activity. Perhaps it would be wise to re-read the chapter on tools before going on to these projects. Please remember that the instructions on how to use tools are meant to be a general outline of how they are to be used. No written instructions can replace lots of practice as a way of learning how to use a tool.

A Wooden Trivet
Made From A Piece Of Scrap Wood

A simple lesson in sanding with the sanding block can produce an attractive wooden trivet.

Materials

One piece of ¾" (2cm) scrap wood,
  approximately 5" x 5" (13 x 13cm)
Sandpaper—80 grit
Scrap felt
Glue

Tools

Sanding block
Scissors

Preparation

Scrap pieces of wood and felt will have to be collected. Since the trivet can be of varying sizes, collecting the wood should be quite easy. Regular pieces of wood do not have to be used for this project: round, trapezoidal, rectangular and triangular pieces will do nicely. The reason for gluing the felt to the bottom is to keep the trivet from marring a table.

In the chapter on Tools, there is a description of how to make a sanding block.

Instructions

1. Using the sanding block, sand all the edges of the piece of wood.

2. Place a piece of felt under the piece of wood and trace around it.

3. Using scissors, cut along the traced line.

4. Glue the felt to the bottom of the piece of wood.

A Tic-Tac-Toe Game
From One Piece Of Scrap Wood

This is a fun game that can be made quite simply and will give children a lot of practice using the hand drill.

Materials

One piece of ¾" (2cm) scrap wood, 4" x 4"
 (10cm x 10cm)
Wooden matches with the firing ends cut off
Magic markers—2 colors
One piece of scrap felt or other material

Tools

Hand drill—3/16" (5mm) bit
Awl or large nail
Pencil
Clamp
Paper punch
Hole spacer (See Preparation)

Preparation

By making the hole spacer in advance, this project will be fun and easy for children.

Trace the hole spacer on a piece of heavy paper. With a paper punch, make holes over the marks. Using this as a guide, make as many hole spacers as you need.

Instructions

1. With the hole spacer placed on the piece of wood, put a pencil mark at each hole.

2. With a nail or awl, make a "starting hole" at each pencil mark.

3. Clamp or hold the piece of wood securely to the table or bench.

4. With the hand drill, drill the nine holes through the piece of wood.

5. Cut the felt to size and glue it to the bottom of the game.

6. Color the match sticks two different colors and the game is ready.

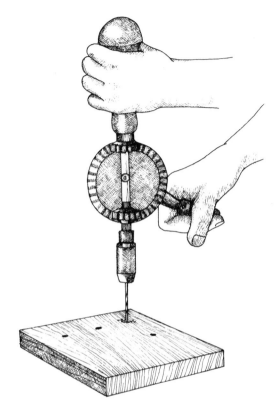

Comments

Children will have to be reminded to hold the hand drill properly. You might want to read the section on the hand drill.

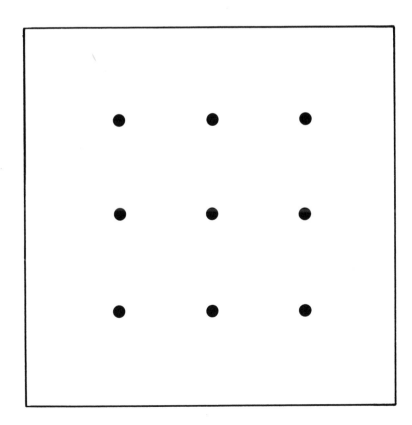

A Tray
Made From A Piece Of Scrap Wood And Some Clothes Line

Children gain practice with the hand drill and learn how to tie an overhand knot.

Materials

A piece of scrap wood approximately
  7½" x 10" (19 x 25cm)
Four 12" (30cm) lengths of lightweight
  clothesline
Glue

Tools

Hand drill—¼" (6cm) bit
Scissors
80 grit sandpaper
1" x 1" (2.5 x 2.5 cm) Measuring Squares
Clamp

Preparation

Measuring squares are made by cutting out squares from heavy paper or cardboard. They make measuring quite simple for younger children. Without the Measuring Squares, it will be necessary for children to use a ruler or a tape measure—tools that are difficult for young children to handle.

¼" (7cm) plywood works well for this project. The size need not be the same as the one suggested. Just make sure that it is of a size that children can handle easily.

The clothesline should be lightweight. Old clothesline works as well as new.

Instructions

1. Put the measuring square in one corner of the piece of wood. Mark a dot at the point of the measuring square that lies within the piece of wood. Do this at all four corners.

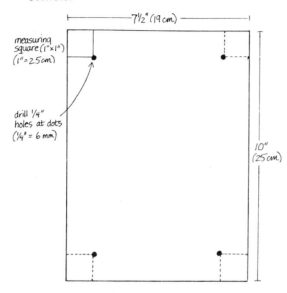

2. Use the hand drill to drill ¼" (7 cm) holes through the dots. Either clamp the wood to the worktable, or have one child hold the wood while the other drills.

3. Sand all the edges of the piece of wood.

4. Tie an overhand knot at the end of one of the pieces of rope. Thread the rope through one hole from the bottom up so the

knot catches under the tray; then put it in the other hole from the top down. Tie another overhand knot on the under side of the tray, making one handle. Do the same thing on the other side of the tray to make the other handle.

5. Cut off any excess rope.

6. Cut two other pieces of rope and glue them to the long edges of the tray. When dry the tray is ready to use.

Comments

Children will need your help in tying the knots. Show them how it is done and let them practice. Make sure that the handles are not made too loose and floppy.

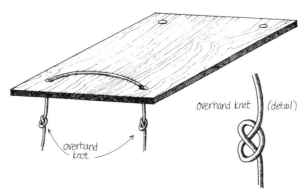

A Musical Sand Block

This instrument is made from two pieces of scrap wood and two empty thread spools. It is easy to make and fun to play.

Materials

Two pieces of ¼" (2cm) scrap wood,
   approximately 3" x 4" (8 x 10cm)
Two empty wooden thread spools
Two pieces of sandpaper, 3" x 4" (8 x 10cm)
Glue

Tools

Scissors

Preparation

Small pieces of scrap wood need to be collected. The exact size is not too important, but each pair needs to be the same size. Have children collect empty thread spools from home.

Instructions

1. Place the wooden pieces over a piece of sandpaper. Trace around them and cut the sandpaper to size.

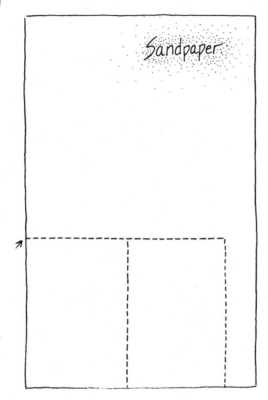

2. Glue the sandpaper to the bottom of the two wooden pieces.

3. Glue an empty thread spool in the center of the two wooden pieces.

4. Paint it, decorate it, use it.

Comments

These sand blocks can be used by children to keep rhythm with a record, or while they sing a song. They lightly brush the two blocks together to the beat of the song. Children will love them—because they made them.

A Musical Wooden Cymbal

This musical instrument is made from two pieces of scrap wood and two empty thread spools.

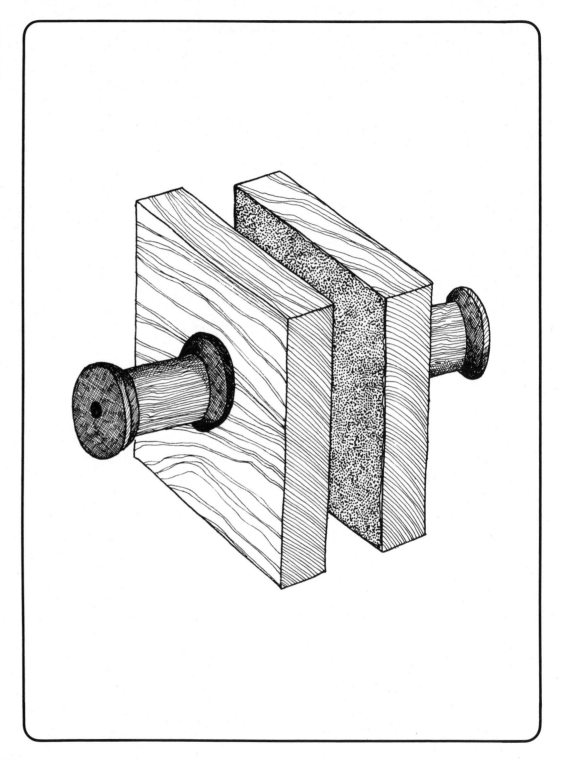

Materials

Two pieces of ¼" (2cm) scrap wood,
  approximately 3" x 4" (8 x 10cm)
Two empty wooden thread spools
Glue

Tools

No tools are necessary

Preparation

Small pieces of scrap wood need to be collected. The exact size is not important, but each pair needs to be the same size. Have children collect empty thread spools from home.

Instructions

1. Glue an empty thread spool in the center of each of the two wooden pieces.

2. After they have dried, they can be painted or decorated with pictures or cut-outs.

Comments

Like the sand blocks, these instruments can be used to keep rhythm with a record or a song.

Bookends
Made From Two Pieces Of Scrap Wood

A fun and easy project using two pieces of scrap wood, a hammer and some glue.

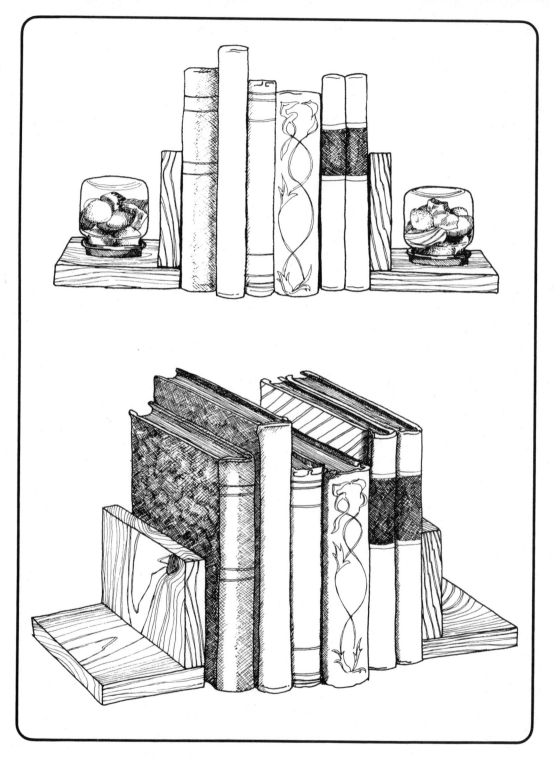

Materials

Two pieces of ¼" (2cm) scrap wood,
   approximately 4" x 5" (10 x 13cm)
1½" (4cm) finishing nails
Non-skid tape
Sandpaper
Glue
Pictures, paints, etc.

Tools

Hammer
Ruler
Pencil

Preparation

   The bookends are attractive without any
painting or pictures, but I've found that
children love to "dress up" their projects.

   It helps if you put non-skid tape on the
bottom of the bookends. It can be purchased
at a drug or hardware store and is
inexpensive. One box of 1½" (4cm)
finishing nails will be enough for a class
project. It is possible to use sizes of wood
other than those described, depending on the
pieces you find. It is important to use soft
wood—fir or pine—as it will be impossible
for children to hammer nails through hard
wood like oak or walnut.

Instructions

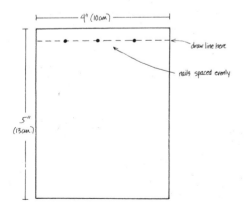

1. Draw a line across the 4" (10cm) side of

two pieces of wood, 3/8" (1cm) from the
edge.

2. Hammer three nails into the pieces of
wood, spacing them evenly along the line.
Hammer them so that they just poke through
the other side.

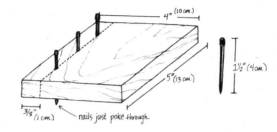

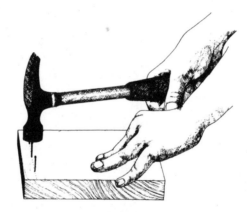

3. Put some glue on the 4" (10cm) edge of
the other pieces of wood.

4. Hold the glued piece of wood upright
and hammer the nailed piece into it. Be sure
you position the wood so that the nails go
into the center of the edge of the other
piece of wood. This step will take two people.
Usually I hold the glued piece of wood and
let the child hammer. Repeat the process
for the other bookend.

5. Put the non-skid tape on the bottom of
the bookends.

6. Sand all the edges.

7. Paint them, glue pictures or photos on
them, and use them.

Comments

This is a simple project, but one that takes
careful attention so that the two pieces of
wood are nailed into the proper position.
The glue makes the wood want to move
around, so it will have to be held securely
until at least two nails are in place. If a nail
is bent, it will have to be removed. Look at
the section on hammering for instructions
on how to remove a nail without damaging
the piece of wood.

   An interesting variation of this project is to
use two babyfood jars, nailing the tops of the
jars to the base of the bookends. The jars can
be used to store some "collectables" and
decorate the bookends at the same time.

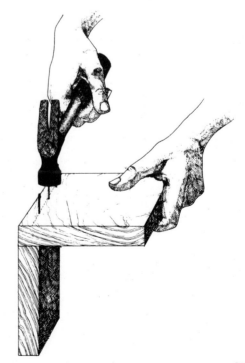

A Note Holder
Made From A Piece Of Scrap Wood And A Clothes Pin

This is a simple and useful project, which will prove to be handy around the house.

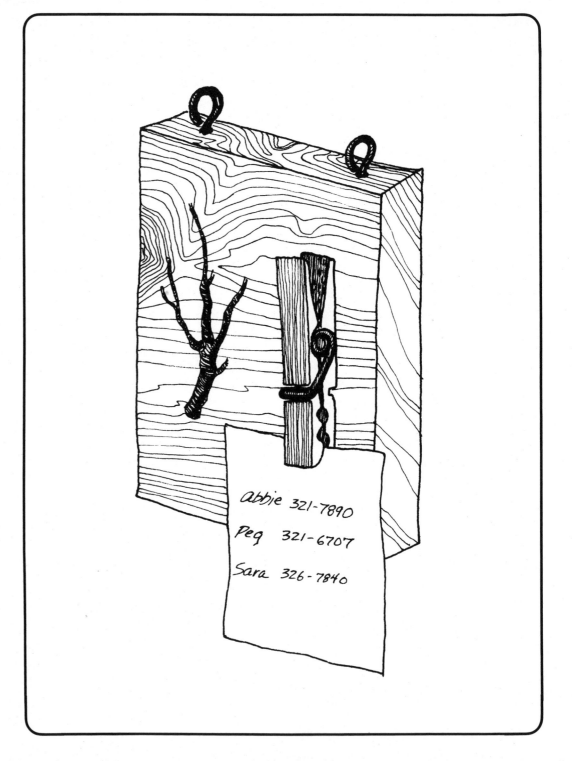

Materials

A piece of scrap wood, approximately
    4" x 5" (10 x 13cm)
A spring-style clothespin
Glue
Cord
Pictures and paint

Tools

Hand drill—3/16" (5cm) bit

Preparation

The exact size of the piece of wood is not too important. You can use several different sizes of wood for this project if you choose. If you are doing the project with small children, you may want to drill the holes before introducing the project, or you may drill them while the children observe.

Clothespins can be found at almost any supermarket.

Instructions

1. Put some glue on the piece of wood where the clothespin will be placed, and some more on the clothespin. Place the glued side of the clothespin on the piece of wood.

2. Let the project dry.

3. Using the hand drill, drill two 3/16" (5mm) holes approximately ½" (12mm) from the top edges.

4. Paint and decorate the holder, if you like. Put some cord through the holes and it is ready to use.

Comments

You may want to glue seeds and sticks or nuts and leaves to the note holder. Almost anything goes well with this project and it quickly becomes a useful part of the home. If you are a parent with several children, you might want to use a larger piece of scrap wood and use several clothespins. Put each person's name below a clothespin and you have a convenient place to leave notes.

A Japanese Serving Table
Made From Three Pieces Of Scrap Wood

This beautiful serving table from Japan is easy to make and looks graceful on the table.

Materials

One piece of ¾" (2cm) scrap wood,
approximately 6" x 9" (15 x 23cm)
Two pieces of ¾" (2cm) scrap wood,
1½" (4cm) wide and 6" (15cm) long
Sandpaper—80 grit
1½" (4cm) finishing nails
Glue

Tools

Hammer
Ruler
Pencil

Preparation

If you purchase the legs for the table,
1" x 2" (3 x 6 cm) pieces of wood can be
found in any lumber yard. They are easy to
cut to the proper length. The back saw and
the miter box can be used to do this. The
top of the table should be approximately
6" x 9" (15 x 23cm). Exact size is not
important. The width should be about two-
thirds of the length.

Instructions

1. With a pencil and ruler, draw a line
2½" (6.5cm) from the edges of the smaller
sides of the piece of wood.

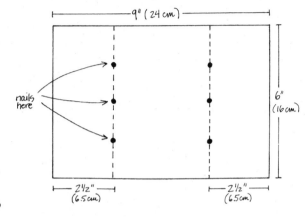

2. Hammer three nails evenly spaced along
each of the lines. Hammer them so that the
nails just poke through the wood.

3. Put some glue on the long edges of the
smaller pieces of wood.

4. Hold the larger piece of wood over the
smaller pieces so that the nails are in the
center of the glued edge.

5. Hammer the pieces of wood together.

6. Wipe off any excess glue with a damp
rag.

7. Sand the edges of the table and it is
ready to use.

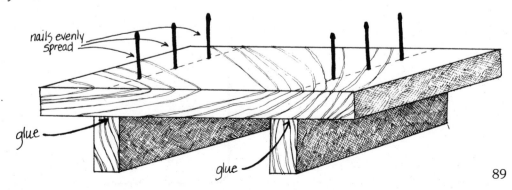

Comments

Vegetable oil can be used to finish the
table. Don't use too much as some vegetable
oils will turn rancid. Peanut oil is best used
for this project. It helps protect the table
and keeps it from splitting.

These are beautiful little tables. The
Japanese serve raw fish, and vegetables
on them with small bowls of soy sauce
and mustard on the side.

89

A Letter Holder
Made From Three Pieces Of Scrap Wood

This is a relatively simple project which makes a beautiful gift.

Materials

Two pieces of ¾" (2cm) wood, 4" x 5" (10 x 13cm)
One piece of ¾" (2cm) wood, 4" (10cm) long and 2" (5cm) wide
Finishing nails—1½" (4cm) long
Glue
Seeds, berries, sticks

Tools

Hammer
Pencil
Ruler

Preparation

Scrap pieces of wood will have to be collected and cut to size. This would be a good project for the local high school shop class. The next two projects will also need their help, so it may be wise to get to know them now.

Sticks, berries and seeds will have to be collected and dried. Perhaps you have some left from the earlier projects.

Instructions

1. Sand all the pieces of wood.

2. Draw a line about ½" (12mm) from the edge of the 4" (10cm) side of the pieces of wood.

3. Hammer the nails evenly along the line so that they just poke through the wood.

4. Put some glue on both of the longer edges of the center piece of wood.

5. Nail the two pieces of wood to the center piece.

6. Glue some seeds, berries, etc. to the front and when dry it is ready to use.

Plywood
Projects

Plywood Projects

Each of the three projects in this chapter uses pieces of one quarter inch (7mm) plywood. Plywood is so named because layers (or ply's) of wood are glued together to make one piece of wood. The grains of the layers are alternated as they are glued together, which greatly increases the strength of the total piece of wood. Because of this, smaller pieces of plywood can be used in place of larger pieces of wood. Plywood is a fairly recent discovery, having been perfected about forty years ago.

The two "hinged" projects use very small pieces of plywood. They should be prepared carefully and cut to be perfectly square, with a hole drilled directly in the middle of one of the pieces. I have found the high school shop class to be an excellent resource in preparing these projects for classroom use. Using very little wood, enough pieces can be prepared in short order for use by an entire class. For home use, the pieces of plywood can be cut out quite simply, but you will need the use of an electric drill to make the holes.

For the children, no woodworking tools are needed to assemble these projects. They will be fascinated with the broom holder.

A Tray
Made From Three Pieces Of Scrap Wood

This is an interesting tray made with no tools other than a pencil and ruler.

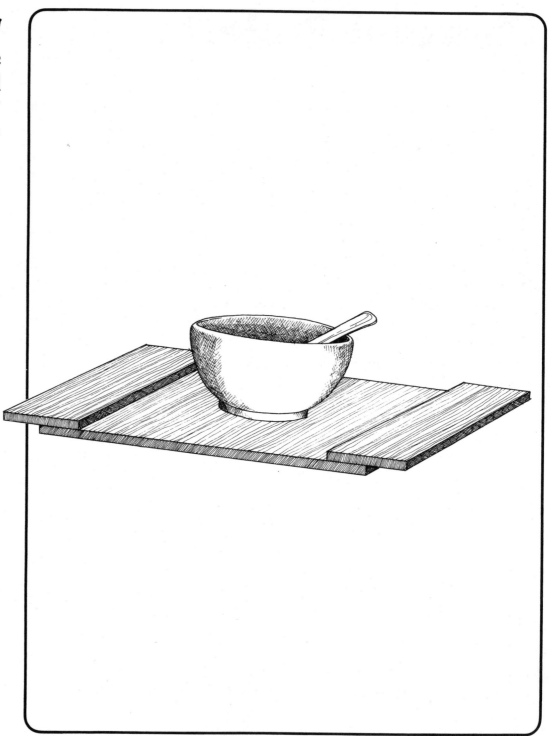

Materials

One piece of scrap wood approximately
   7½" x 10" (19 x 25cm)
Two pieces of scrap wood, each
   approximately 2½" (6cm) wide and 7½"
   (19cm) long.
Sandpaper—80 grit
Glue
Masking tape

Tools

Ruler
Pencil

Preparation

The thickness of the wood is not too
important. I've found ¼" (7mm) plywood
works quite well. The "handles" of the tray
can easily be cut from one by three inch wood
if you can't find any scrap wood that is
usable.

Instructions

1. Sand all the edges with 80 grit sandpaper.

2. Lay the ruler along the edge of the shorter
side of the large piece of wood. Draw a line
on the inside edge of the ruler. Repeat this
on the other side of the wood.

3. Put some glue on the smaller pieces.

4. Lay them on the larger piece of wood so
that one edge lies along the pencil line and
the other protrudes over the edge.

5. Put masking tape along the edges to hold
the pieces of wood in place while they dry.

6. Make sure you wipe any extra glue with a
damp rag.

Comments

To make a fancy tray you may want to
use a picture or a piece of paper lace. Glue
it to the top of the tray and after drying,
varnish the entire project.

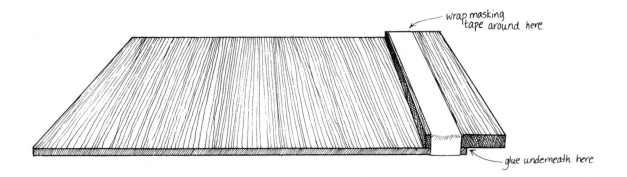

wrap masking tape around here

glue underneath here

A Photo Hinge

Besides making an attractive frame,
this project provides a simple
explanation of the hinge.

Materials

Two ¼" (7mm) plywood squares, 3" x 3"
   (7.5 x 7.5cm). One of the squares has a
   1" (2.5cm) hole drilled in the center of it.
Scrap cloth or leather (old blue jeans work
   well) 2" x 3" (5 x 7.5cm)
Glue
Sand paper—120 grit
Waxed paper
Photo of child

Tools

Scissors

Preparation

The plywood squares will have to be cut to
size and have holes drilled in them before the
project is introduced to children. Try to have
a good number of these prepared at the same
time. The same pieces are used in the next
project and are good to have around for that
child who needs a project "now!"

Old jeans are made of tough material
which works well to make these hinges. If
you can find some scrap leather, it makes
beautiful hinges.

A photo of each child doing this project
is also necessary.

Instructions

1. Put a piece of waxed paper on the work
table to protect it from the glue, and to
prohibit the project from being glued to the
work table.

2. Cut out a small piece of fabric 3" x 2"
(7.5cm x 5cm)

3. Put some glue on the fabric. Saturate it
well. Lay it on the waxed paper, glued side
up.

4. Put some glue on the wooden squares.
Position them so that they are next to one
another and centered over the piece of fabric.
Push on them to make sure they adhere to
the fabric. Put something on top of the
squares and allow them to dry for four hours.

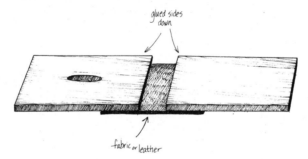

5. After the photo hinge has dried, sand it
and glue a photo on the inside.

Comments

Some time ago I became fascinated with
the hinge as a means of connecting pieces of
wood together without using any hardware.
Using fabric or leather makes an
exceptionally strong hinge, yet is soft and
costs next to nothing. This photo hinge
makes a wonderful gift to give to
grandparents.

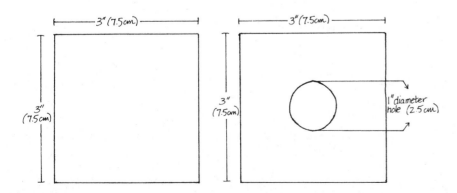

The Magic Broom Holder

This project got its name because it works like magic. My father sent me the inspiration for it. He said he made it when he was a child. It really does work like magic.

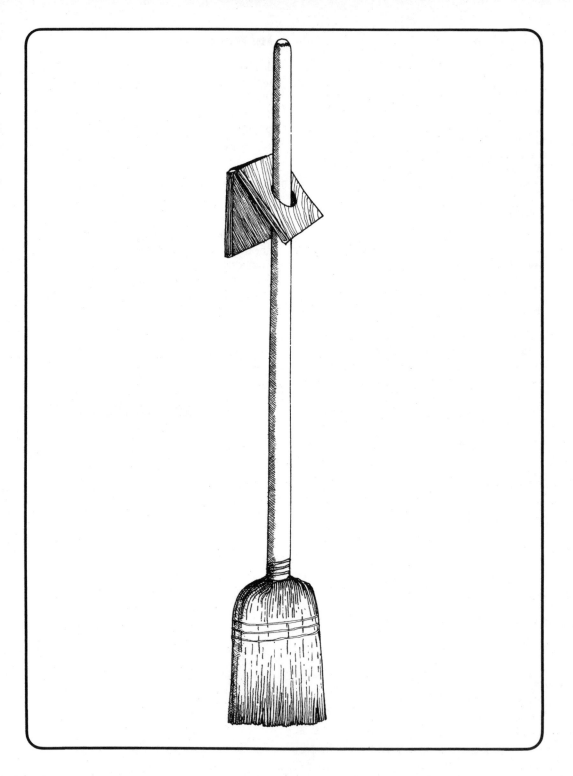

Materials

Two ¼" (7mm) plywood squares, 3" x 3"
(7.5 x 7.5cm). One of the squares has a
1" (2.5cm) hole drilled in the center of it.
Scrap cloth or leather (old blue jeans work
well)
One 5/8" (15mm) screw
Glue
Sandpaper—120 grit
Waxed paper

Tools

Scissors

Preparation

The preparation for this project is
virtually the same as for the preceeding one.
If you cut out enough squares the last time,
there will be no preparation needed for this
project.

Instructions

1. Cut out a small piece of fabric 3" x 4"
(7.5 x 10cm). Note that this is a larger piece
of fabric than that used for the hinged
photo.

2. Put a piece of waxed paper on the work
table to protect its surface and keep the
project from becoming glued to it.

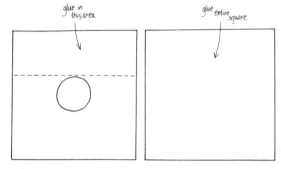

3. Put glue on one side of the square without
the hole. Put glue on the top part of the
square with the hole.

4. Lay the square without the hole on the
waxed paper, *glued side up*. Now place the
fabric over this square, and put the square
with the hole next to it, *glued side down*.
Push on the fabric and squares to make sure
they bond well. Put something heavy over
the project and let it dry for four hours.

5. After the broom holder has dried it is ready
to be hung with the 5/8" (15mm) screw.

Comments

Although this is a simple project, it requires
careful attention to line up the two squares
so that they make a good hinge. Don't spare
the glue.

Children will love this after it is hung up.
Perhaps you can make a few for the
classroom. I keep one in my shop with a
sawed off broom in it. Part of every project
is cleaning up afterwards, and the children
who work with me have a special broom in
a magic broom holder for doing that job.

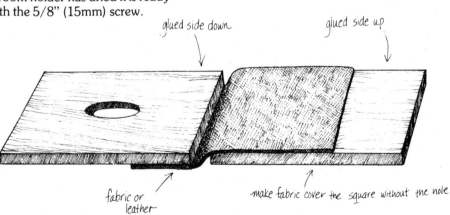

Three
Advanced
Projects

Three Advanced Projects

Time flies like the wind. We started with writing our names with sticks and now we are building toolboxes. Yet, even in the final projects, sticks are used. These final three projects have been chosen because they build on the experiences and skills learned in the earlier ones. The hanging plant holder is built like the card holder with two additional pieces of wood. The birdhouse is built like two bookends nailed together. The toolbox is built from one piece of wood cut into five pieces.

I've kept the preparation for these projects to a minimum. The toolbox is the only project in the book that involves cutting wood at an angle. The rest of the projects involve only straight cuts. The plant holder and the birdhouse each have only two different sizes of wood. The toolbox has three. If you have an available friend or are using the facilities of the high school shop, the preparation will be very simple. If you are cutting out the pieces yourself, you will need no other tools than a hand saw and a hand drill. Of course, if you have an electric skill saw and an electric drill, the preparation will be even easier.

There are many more wonderful experiences to explore with wood. I wish we didn't have to stop here, but we do. Thank you for sharing in this experience.

A Flower Pot Holder

Made From Five Pieces Of Wood

This is a beautiful project, easier to make than it looks.

Materials

Four pieces of ¾" (2cm) wood, 3" x 5"
   (7.5cm x 12.5cm)
One piece of ¾" (2cm) wood, 3" x 3½"
   (7.5cm x 8.8cm)
One stick, approximately ¼" (6mm) thick
   and 7" (18cm) long
Finishing nails—1½" (4cm)
Glue
Sandpaper—80 grit
Cord

Tools

Ruler
Hammer
Hand Drill—¼" (6mm) bit
Awl
Pencil

Preparation

In this project, as in the next two, exact measurements are important. The wood will have to be cut out by an adult. As you become more familiar with the project you can alter the measurements, as long as the bottom piece is the same width as the side pieces, and its length is 1½" (38mm) shorter than the side pieces.

The sticks in this project should be straight.

Instructions

1. Glue and nail two of the side pieces to the bottom piece.

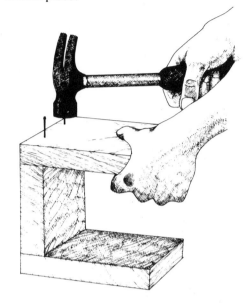

2. Glue and nail the other two side pieces.

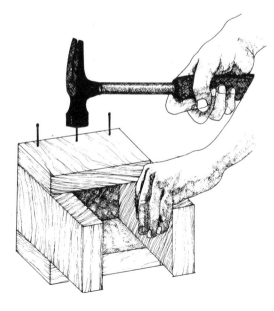

3. With a hammer and a large nail mark a starting hole in each of the two sides.

4. Using the hand drill and a ¼" (7mm) bit, drill a hole at the mark in each of the two sides.

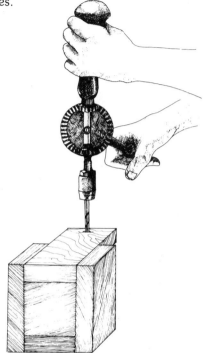

5. Put a stick through the holes.

6. Sand the project and put a protective coating on it.

7. Tie a cord around the stick and it is ready to use.

Comments

Of all the projects in this book, I think this one is the most beautiful. You can alter the dimensions while still retaining the basic form. If using redwood or cedar, I would suggest putting no finish on the wood, allowing it to take on the color of wood aged naturally by water and sun.

A Birdhouse

This is a project based on the skills learned in making the bookends.

Materials

Four pieces of ¾" (2cm) wood, 5½" x 5½"
  (14 x 14cm)
Two pieces of ¾" (2cm) wood, 4¾" x 4¾"
  (12 x 12cm)
One stick, approximately ¼" (7mm) thick
  and 3½" (9cm) long
Finishing nails—1½" (4cm)
Glue
Sandpaper
Two screw eyes
Cord

Tools

Hammer
Awl
Hand Drill—¼" (6mm) bit
Pencil

Preparation

Four of the pieces of wood are of one
size, two are of another size. All can be cut
from a standard piece of 1" x 6" (2 x 14.5cm)
fir or pine. Note that the *actual* size of each
piece of wood is not one inch (2.5cm) thick
and six inches (15cm) wide, but ¾" (2cm)
thick and 5½" (14cm) wide.

One of the smaller pieces should have a
hole drilled in its center, ¾" (2cm) in
diameter. This can be done with a hand drill,
but goes much faster with an electric drill.
The hole for the stick perch can be drilled by
the children.

Sticks, sandpaper, eyelets, cord and glue
will have to be collected.

Perhaps it would be wise to reread the
bookends project (page 124) as the initial
pieces of wood are assembled in the same
way as in that project.

Also, be sure to use aliphatic resin (yellow)
glue, as the birdhouse will be out of doors.

For finishing the project, read the section
on finishing.

Instructions

1. With pencil and ruler, draw a line 3/8"
(1cm) from the edge of one side of each of
the four larger pieces of wood.

2. Hammer three nails evenly spaced along
each of the four lines so that the nails just
poke through the wood.

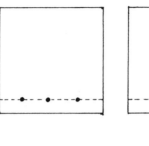 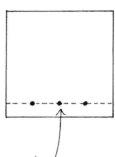 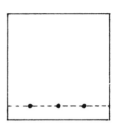 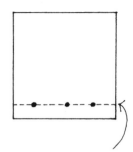

Hammer nails evenly spread along each of the four lines so that the nails just poke through the wood

Draw lines 3/8" (1cm) from the edge of each of the four larger pieces

3. Take two pieces, glue and hammer them
together. Do the same with the other two
pieces.

109

4. Now hammer the two pairs of wood together.

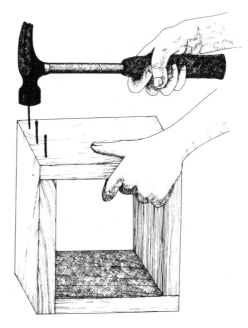

5. Now you have a square. Put some glue on the edges of the smaller two pieces of wood and fit them into the two ends of the square. If they do not fit snugly enough, use nails to secure the ends to the square.

6. When dry, drill a hole just below the large opening for the bird and fit in a stick as the perch.

7. Put in the two eyelets, tie a cord between them and the birdhouse is ready to finish and hang.

8. For finishing, read the section on Finishing.

Comments

There are a lot of ways to make a birdhouse. This is but one. I like it because it uses only two sizes of wood, making the preparation fairly easy. It also gives a slant to the roof while still using straight pieces of wood. As your children become more experienced in woodworking, they will come up with all sorts of designs.

A Toolbox

This is the final project in this book...a useful box for a young woodworker.

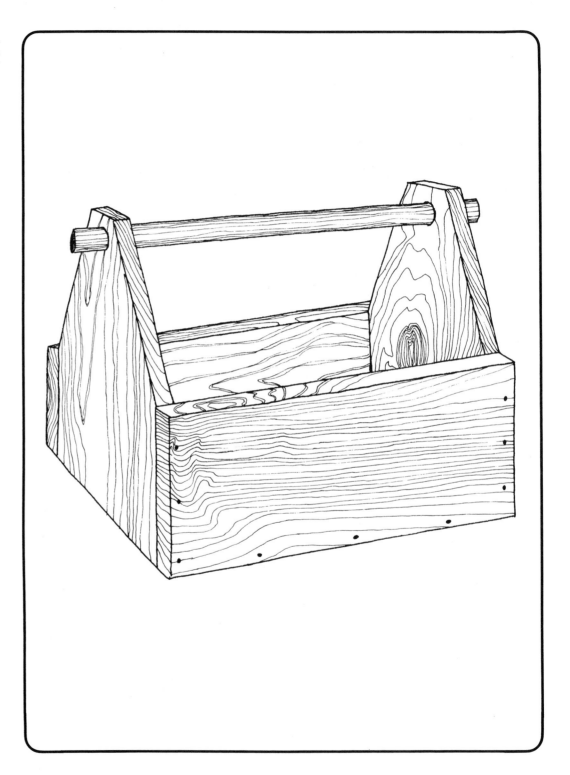

Materials

Two pieces of ¾" (2cm) wood, 5½" x 13"
   (14 x 33cm)
Two pieces of ¾" (2cm) wood, 5½" x 11"
   (14 x 28cm)
One piece of ¾" (2cm) wood, 5½" x 11½"
   (14 x 29.2cm)
One dowel, ¾" (2cm) x 15" (38cm)
Finishing nails 1½" (4cm)
Glue
Sandpaper—80 grit

Tools

Hammer
Pencil
Ruler

Preparation

   This is the only project that involves cutting
pieces of wood at angles. Each toolbox uses
about five feet (150cm) of wood. All of the
pieces are cut from a standard piece of 1" x 6"
(2 x 14.5cm) fir or pine. They can be cut
with a hand saw or a power saw depending
upon what resources are available to you.
Study the diagram below to see how to cut
the pieces to their correct dimensions. Once
in a while I find a child who is ready to use
a hand saw and can make these cuts. By
and large, however, it will have to be done
by an adult. I doubt if this will be a project
that will be done by an entire class.

   The holes for the handle will have to be
drilled. If you have a real sharp bit, a child
may be able to use a hand drill to drill these
holes. I find it better to either drill the holes
beforehand using an electric drill, or do the
drilling as a demonstration with the children
observing. The diagram below shows where
to locate the holes.

Instructions

1. With pencil and ruler, draw a line 3/8"
(1cm) from the bottom edge of the two end
pieces. Also draw lines along three edges of
the two side pieces.

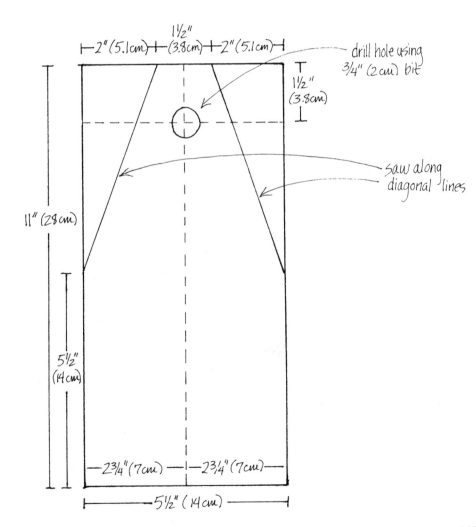

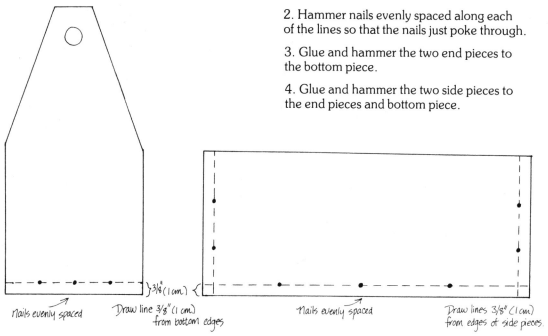

Nails evenly spaced

Draw line 3/8" (1 cm) from bottom edges

Nails evenly spaced

Draw lines 3/8" (1 cm) from edges of side pieces.

2. Hammer nails evenly spaced along each of the lines so that the nails just poke through.

3. Glue and hammer the two end pieces to the bottom piece.

4. Glue and hammer the two side pieces to the end pieces and bottom piece.

Comments

Unlike the more decorative projects, this one is likely to get a lot of use. I'd suggest finishing the toolbox with two coats of whatever finish you choose.

If the box is made for a specialized use, the dimensions can, of course, be altered.

A stick, about the size of the dowel can be used in its place. It is a little difficult to find one the correct size and making it fit will most likely entail some extra steps, but the box becomes very personal (and very beautiful).

5. Insert the dowel and hammer a nail into the dowel from the top of the end pieces.

6. Sand the toolbox and it is ready to finish. See the section on finishing.

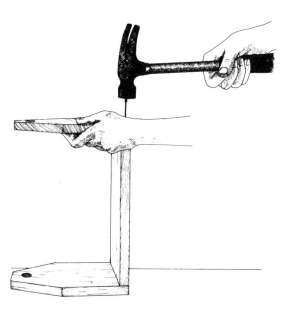

Guardians of our forests
Guardians of our children
We learn as we love.